PREFACE.

The Society of Friends has numbered within its ranks many eminent women, who have enunciated and explained its doctrines and testimonies, both by their ministry and writings; and have illustrated its Christian faith by the consistency of their lives and conversation, and their patience under persecution. Amongst these, none shone more conspicuously, in the early days of the Society, than the subject of this memoir. Having been convinced by the baptizing ministry of George Fox, she became a faithful member of the church; her influence and reputation in the community, as well as her ministry and writings, greatly contributing to advance the cause of truth. As a preacher of the Gospel, she was fervent and weighty; as a writer, bold, earnest and persuasive;

in her disposition, charitable and hospitable; and a warm sympathizer with the afflicted and persecuted.

Her works having been long out of print, and almost unknown in this country, it is believed that the following compilation, giving a brief account of her life, a selection from her epistles, and a few extracts from her other writings, will prove acceptable to the reader.

THE LIFE

OF

MARGARET FOX.

WIFE OF GEORGE FOX.

COMPILED FROM HER OWN NARRATIVE, AND OTHER SOURCES;

WITH A

SELECTION FROM HER EPISTLES, ETC.

PHILADELPHIA:
PUBLISHED BY THE
ASSOCIATION OF FRIENDS FOR THE DIFFUSION OF RELIGIOUS
AND USEFUL KNOWLEDGE,
109 NORTH TENTH STREET.
1859.

LIFE

OF

MARGARET FOX.

CHAPTER I. 1614–1658.

HER BIRTH—PARENTAGE—MARRIES THOMAS FELL, AND SETTLES AT SWARTHMORE — RELIGIOUS LIFE — VISITED BY GEORGE FOX — SHE AND HER CHILDREN CONVINCED — DISPLEASURE OF HER HUSBAND—LETTER FROM R. FARNSWORTH — JUDGE FELL RECONCILED, AND A MEETING ESTABLISHED AT HER HOUSE — TESTIMONY OF A. PIERSON AND WILLIAM CATON TO THE EXEMPLARY CHARACTER OF THE FAMILY — DEATH OF HER HUSBAND — HIS CHARACTER — LETTER OF CONDOLENCE FROM A. PIERSON — THEIR CHILDREN.

MARGARET FOX was born at Marsh Grange, in the parish of Dalton, in Fournis, Lancashire, England, in the year 1614. She was the daughter of John Askew, who was of an ancient and honourable family; he was honest, pious and charitable, and a man of estate and education.

She was married, in her eighteenth year, to Thomas Fell, of Swarthmore, a barrister-at-law, afterwards a justice of the Quorum in his county, a member of several Parliaments, vice-chancellor of the county Palatine of Lancaster, and also a judge in the circuit of West Chester and North Wales, &c. Strict integrity and love of justice, tempered with mercy and moderation, were conspicuous traits in his character.

In the seventy-sixth year of her age she wrote a short biographical sketch, rehearsing some of the principal events of her life, which has been largely used in the preparation of this work; in which, speaking of her husband, she says:—"We lived together twenty-six years, in which time we had nine children. He was a tender and loving husband to me, and a tender father to his children, and one that sought after God in the best way that was made known to him. I was about sixteen years younger than he, and was one that sought after the best things, being desirous to serve God, so that I might be accepted of Him; and was inquiring after the way of the Lord, and went often to hear the best ministers that came into our parts, whom we frequently entertained at our house; many of those that were accounted the most serious, godly men, some of whom we then called lecturing ministers; and often had prayers and religious exercises in our family. This I hoped I did well in, but often feared I was short of the right way; and after this manner I was inquiring and seeking about twenty years, when, in 1652, it pleased the Lord, in his infinite mercy and goodness, to send George Fox into our country, who declared unto us the eternal truth, as it is in Jesus; and by the Word and power of the eternal God.

turned many from darkness unto light, and from the power of Satan unto God."

The powerful and awakening nature of the spiritual ministry of George Fox, and the effect produced by it on her own mind, and his discourse on this occasion, she thus describes: —

"Our house being a place open to entertain ministers and religious people, one of George Fox's friends brought him thither, where he staid all night; and the next day being a lecture or fast-day, he went to Ulverstone steeple-house, but came not in till people were gathered; I and my children had been a long time there before. And when they were singing, before the sermon, he came in; and when they had done, he stood up, upon a seat or form, and desired 'that he might have liberty to speak;' and he that was in the pulpit said he might. And the first words that he spoke were as followeth: 'He is not a Jew that is one outward, neither is that circumcision which is outward; but he is a Jew that is one inward, and that is circumcision which is of the heart.' And so he went on and said 'that Christ was the light of the world, and lighteth every man that cometh into the world; and that by this light they might be gathered to God,' &c. I stood up in my pew, and wondered at his doctrine; for I had never heard such before: and then he went on, and opened the Scriptures, and said: 'The Scriptures were the prophet's words, and Christ's and the apostles' words; and what, as they spoke, they enjoyed and possessed, and had it from the Lord:' and said:

'Then what had any to do with the Scriptures, but as they came to the spirit that gave them forth. You will say Christ saith this, and the apostles say this; but what canst *thou* say? Art *thou* a child of light, and hast walked in the light; and what thou speaketh, is it inwardly from God,' &c. This opened me so, that it cut me to the heart; and then I saw clearly we were all wrong. So I sat down in my pew again, and cried bitterly; and I cried in my spirit to the Lord: 'We are all thieves; we are all thieves;* we have taken the Scriptures in words, and know nothing of them in ourselves.' So that served me, that I cannot well tell what he spoke afterwards; but he went on declaring against false prophets, priests and deceivers of the people. And he came to our house again that night, and spoke in the family amongst the servants, and they were all generally convinced. And I was struck into such sadness, I knew not what to do, my husband being from home. I saw it was the truth, and I could not deny it; and I did as the apostle saith: 'I received the truth in the love of it;' and it was opened to me so clear, that I had never a tittle in my heart against it; but I desired the Lord that I might be kept in it, and then I desired no greater portion."

George Fox, in describing the circumstances attending his visit to Swarthmore at this time, after

* Probably in allusion to John x. 1: "Verily, verily, I say unto you, he that entereth not by the door into the sheepfold, but climbeth up some other way, the same is a thief and a robber."

relating his controversies with the parish priest, Lampitt, and his discourses on religious subjects with M. Fell and her children, in which they were measurably convinced, says that, "soon after, a day was to be observed for a humiliation; and Margaret Fell asked me to go with her to the steeple-house at Ulverstone, for she was not wholly come off from them. I replied: 'I must do as I am ordered of the Lord. So I left her, and walked into the fields; and the word of the Lord came unto me, saying: 'Go to the steeple-house after them.' When I came, Lampitt was singing with his people; but his spirit was so foul, and the matter they sung so unsuitable to their states, that after they had done singing, I was moved of the Lord to speak to him and the people. Then, as the Lord opened further, I showed them that He was come to teach His people by his spirit, and to bring them off from their old ways, religions, churches and worships; for all their religions, worships and ways were but taking other men's words; but they were out of the life and spirit which those were in who gave them forth. Then cried out one Justice Sawrey: 'Take him away;' but Judge Fell's wife said to the officers: 'Let him alone; why may he not speak, as well as any other?' Lampitt, also, the priest, in deceit said: 'Let him speak.' So at length, when I had declared a pretty while, Justice Sawrey caused the constable to put me out; and then I spake to the people in the grave-yard."

Margaret Fell continues: "And when I and my children, and a great part of our servants, were so convinced and converted unto God, my husband was not at home, being gone to London. When he came home, and found us the most part of his family changed from our former principles and persuasions, which he left us in, he was much surprised at our sudden change; for some envious people, our neighbours, went and met him, and informed him that we had entertained such men as had taken us off from going to church, which he was very much concerned at, and seemed much troubled.

And it so happened that Richard Farnsworth, and some other Friends (that came into our parts a little after George Fox), were then at our house; and they discoursed with him, and did persuade him to be still, and weigh things before he did anything hastily, and his spirit was somewhat calmed. And after he had heard them speak awhile, he was better satisfied. I desired them to stay, and not go away, for George Fox will come this evening. And I would have had my husband to have heard them all, and satisfied himself further about them, because they had so prepossessed him against them, of such dangerous, fearful things. And then he was pretty moderate and quiet; and his dinner being ready, he went to it, and I went in and sat me down by him. And whilst I was sitting, the power of the Lord seized upon me; and he was struck with amazement, and knew not what to think. And the children were all quiet and still, and grown sober, and could not play on their music, that they were learning; and all these things made him quiet."

"At night, George Fox came; and after supper, as my husband was sitting in the parlor, I asked if he might come in? and he said 'Yes.' So George, without any compliment, walked into the room, and began to speak presently; and the family, and James Naylor, and Richard Farnsworth, came in; and he spoke very excellently, as ever I heard him, and opened Christ's and the apostle's practices: and if all England had been there, I thought they could not deny the truth of these things."

George Fox relates: "Soon after Judge Fell being come home, Margaret his wife desiring me to return thither, and I feeling freedom of the Lord so to do, went back to Swarthmore. I found the priests, and professors, and Justice Sawrey, had much incensed Judge Fell and Captain Sands against the truth by their lies; I answered all his objections, and so thoroughly satisfied him by the Scriptures, that he was convinced in his judgment. After we had discoursed a pretty while together, he was satisfied, and came to see, by the openings of the spirit of God in his heart, over all the priests and teachers in the world, and did not go to hear them for some years before he died; for he knew it was the truth I declared, and that Christ was the teacher of his people, and their Saviour."

The following letter, addressed to Margaret Fell by Richard Farnsworth, a few months after, may serve to show the continued interest he took in her convincement and establishment in the truth: —

"*Balbie, Yorkshire, 12th month,* 1652.

DEAR SISTER:—

Mind to stand in the council of the Lord, which will keep down everything that would be exalted, and will not suffer thee to conform to anything but that which is pure. Oh! be faithful, be faithful to what thou knowest; and stand perfect in the will of the Lord; and the Lord will keep thee, in His own power to Himself, and arm thee every way with His love and power. Stand in His council, and it will discover all the consultations of the enemy; and will scatter all imaginations, and will not suffer them to take place in thee, being but obedient to Him. Love not the world, but mind that which would draw thee to live in the pure obedience of Him who is pure; and standing in the pure fear, it will take away all slavish fears, and it will not suffer thee to conform to the world in anything; but thou wilt be preserved in obedience to the Lord in what he doth require; for the fear of the Lord keepeth the heart clean; and it will keep thee clean, and open to receive the teachings of the Father. Oh! stand fast in the liberty wherewith Christ has set thee free, and it will keep thee from the entanglements of the world; and thy preservation will be, in standing in the council of the Lord, who is the mighty Counsellor, the everlasting Prince of peace; who will lead thee and guide thee into the everlasting kingdom of the Father, where there is peace and joy, rest, quietness and assurance forever! Give thyself up wholly to the Lord, who will preserve thee in faithfulness and purity; and the everlasting Lord God Almighty keep thee, and all the rest of our dear Friends, in the power of His love, and in the power of His truth, perfect in His will; that ye may grow from strength to strength, and be established in the everlasting truth; and that He alone may be glorified, who is Lord of lords, and King of kings; to whom be glory, and honour, and praise, and thanks, for ever and ever! Amen.

I received thy letter, which did much rejoice me. When thy letter, with James and George, came, I was then gone towards Derbyshire, where I met with a gathered church. I have been in much service since I came from you. Friends are much emboldened and courageous, who have had great opposition and persecution here away; but all is at a stand; the enemy is much in silence; and the Lord carries on His own work, much to His own praise; to Him alone be glory, and honour, for ever and ever!

My dear, love in the Lord presents itself to you all, to thy son George, and to thy daughters, and to all those thy servants in the truth of God; and the Lord cause them all to grow up into the truth, that He may be exalted amongst you all. Ah! my dear hearts, prize the love and mercy of the Lord, and daily mind your growth into that which is eternal; and the everlasting love and power of the Lord keep you all in faithfulness to Him in what you know. Keep in the cross, and purity will grow. The safest way is in the cross; take up the cross daily; mind to be guided by that which crosseth your own wills, and it will bring every idle word, thought and deed to judgment in you; and so the old man will be crucified, with the affections and lusts thereof; and you shall find the Lord to sit as a refiner, to judge out all the old leaven, the old nature; and so the new man will be raised up; and Christ, the power of God, will rule and reign in righteousness in you, who is the King of saints; to Him alone be all praise and thanks forevermore! Amen!"

Although Judge Fell did not openly unite with Friends, or attend their meetings, he was very favourable to their views, and generally sat in an adjoining room, where he could hear, without appearing to join in their worship. Some Friends, in his presence, speaking of the difficulty in obtaining a place to hold their meetings in that part of the country, he promptly and generously offered them his own house, saying: "You may meet here, if you will;" and notice being given, "there was a good large meeting there the next first-day," which was the first held at Swarthmore, where a meeting was established, and continued from 1652 to 1690. The room appropriated for this purpose was the large hall on the ground-floor, at one end of which, within the space of a bay window, the floor is raised two steps. In this place, it is said, George Fox and his wife usually took their seats, and the other ministering Friends, when present. From this window George

Fox often preached to the people assembled in the adjoining orchard, when they were unable, from their numbers, to meet within.

George Fox's fame, spreading with his doctrine, usually caused a large company to assemble to hear him, when he visited Swarthmore. At one time, Judge Fell, upon returning home, finding his stables filled with the horses of these strange guests, complained to his wife of the large accession of new comers, saying, if this continued, they would soon be eaten out, and have no provender left for themselves. To this she pleasantly replied, that *charity doth not impoverish;* and notwithstanding all this extra consumption, she fully believed that, at the end of the year, he would have no cause to regret their hospitality. And so it proved, for the same year the crop of hay was so abundant, that they had not only plenty for themselves, but a large surplus to sell.

The example of this excellent family doubtless exercised a powerful influence on the minds of many who came within the sphere of its influence, inviting them to come taste and handle for themselves of the good Word of life, of which they had been made partakers, by yielding obedience to the requirings of truth. Several of their household became preachers of righteousness in word and conversation, and were instrumental in turning many from darkness to light, and from the power of Satan to God. Anthony Pierson, in a letter dated in 1653, thus describes the impressions which a visit to Swarthmore produced on his mind: "Oh! how gracious the Lord was to me in carrying me to Judge Fell's, to see the wonders of His power and wisdom; a family walking in the fear of the Lord, conversing daily with Him, crucified to the world, and living only to God. I was so confounded, all my knowledge and wisdom became folly; my mouth was stopped, my conscience convinced, and the secrets of my heart were made manifest, and that Lord was discovered to be near, whom I ignorantly worshipped. I have seen at Judge Fell's, and have been informed from that precious soul his consort, in some measure what those things mean, which before I counted the overflowing of giddy brains. Dear heart, pity and pray for me, and let all obligations of former friendship be discharged, in well wishes to the soul of the old family friend, that he may partake with them of your heavenly possession."

In confirmation of this, is the testimony of William Caton, an inmate of the family. He says: —

"Oh! the love which in that day abounded among us, especially in that family! and oh! the freshness of the power of the Lord God, which then was amongst us; and the zeal for Him and His truth, the comfort and refreshment which we had from His presence, the nearness and dearness that was amongst us one towards another, the openings and revelations which we then had! my heart is affected with the remembrance of them at this very day. And hence came that worthy family to be so renowned in the nation, the fame of which spread much among Friends; and the power and presence of the Lord being so much there with us, it was as a means to induce many, even from afar, to come thither; so that at one time there would have been Friends out of five or six counties: all which tended to the augmenting of my refreshment. And on the other hand was I cherished and encouraged in the way of life, by my entirely beloved friend Margaret Fell, who as a tender-hearted nursing mother cared for me, and was as tender of me, as if I had been one of her own children. Oh! the kindness, the respect and friendship which she showed me, ought never to be forgotten by me."

Margaret Fell continues, speaking of her husband: "He lived about six years after I was convinced, in which time it pleased the Lord to visit him with sickness, wherein he became more than usually loving and kind to our friends called Quakers, having been a merciful man to the Lord's people. I and many other Friends were well satisfied, the Lord in mercy received him to Himself."

His death occurred in the eighth month, 1658, he being about sixty years of age, leaving one son and seven daughters.*

---

* The son's name was George; the daughters, Margaret, married to John Rous; Sarah, to William Mead; Mary, to Thomas Lower; Susanna, to William Ingram; Rachel, to Daniel Abraham; Isabel, to —— Yeomans, afterwards to Abraham Morris; and Bridget, to John Draper. These marriages all occurred after his death.

John Rous suffered severe persecutions in New England, and in addition to many cruel whippings, had his right ear

William Penn, speaking of him, says: "Being a just and wise man, and seeing in his own wife and family a full confutation of all the popular clamors against the way of truth, he covered them what he could, and freely opened his doors, and gave up his house to his wife and her friends, not valuing the reproach of ignorant or evil-minded people; which I here mention to his and her honour. That house was, for some years at first, till the truth had opened its way in the southern parts of the island, an eminent receptacle of this people."

Alexander Parker thus condoles with her on the death of her husband, and bears testimony to his worth: "Dear Sister, be thou comforted and refreshed; though an outward stay be taken from thee, the Lord, I know, will never leave thee nor forsake thee: thy house is not left desolate, but the God of Jacob will be thy refuge, and the Lord thy Maker is thy husband. It was but very lately I heard of the laying down of the body of thy husband, and truly it did at first sadden my spirit, knowing his dear love and tender care over the Lord's lambs."

---

cut off. He was a native of Barbadoes, subsequently settled near London. William Mead was the companion of William Penn at the time of their persecution and celebrated trial at the Old Baily, familiar to all readers of Friends' history.

CHAPTER II. 1658–1662.

LETTERS TO CROMWELL — LETTER FROM A. RIGGE — GEORGE FOX APPREHENDED AT HER HOUSE — HER ACCOUNT OF HIS APPREHENSION—GOES TO LONDON—INTERVIEW WITH KING CHARLES II. — LETTER AND ADDRESSES TO HIM AND THE PARLIAMENT — INSURRECTION OF THE FIFTH MONARCHY MEN — SOLICITS AND OBTAINS THE DISCHARGE OF G. FOX—SEVERAL LETTERS TO THE KING, DUKE OF YORK, ETC.—VISITS COL. HACKER IN PRISON—LETTER TO HER CHILDREN — RETURNS TO LONDON — ANOTHER INTERVIEW WITH THE KING RESPECTING THE IMPRISONMENT OF FRIENDS — RETURNS HOME — LETTER TO THE KING — LETTER FROM F. HOWGILL.

THIS devoted woman, soon after her convincement, felt called to plead the cause of the persecuted and oppressed before the rulers of the land. She fearlessly approached the monarchs, and those in power, at various times during the course of her life, and laid before them the sufferings of Friends, explained their principles, and both by word and writing warned them of the consequences that would be likely to follow; that the righteous judgments of the Lord would be against such, who were persecuting others for conscience' sake. Her services in this way were of the most persevering and undaunted kind, and manifested her to be one in spirit and courage with her friend, George Fox. About this period, she addressed four letters to the Protector,

Oliver Cromwell; in the second, she "bears witness to the spiritual worship of God, and to His mighty day, and teaching of His people Himself, and against all the outward formal worships which are without the spirit of truth, and of their overthrow; and against all the dark forms, and shadows, and false coverings, which he had been under; charging him, in the presence of God, not to give way to the men of the world, to make laws over the consciences of his servants, and to beware of hearkening to evil counsellors, that would make a prey upon the people for their own ends, lest he brought guilt, plagues, and woe upon himself."

Ambrose Rigge thus bears testimony to the usefulness and worth of M. Fell, at this time, in the church:—

'*Binscombe, in Surry*, 9*th mo.* (11*th mo.*), 1659.

DEAR SISTER—

Often art thou in my remembrance, in my labour and travel in the vineyard of the Lord, which is grown sweet and pleasant to walk in, to the praise of God. I received thy lines in Hampshire, when I was in much weakness of body, by which I was much strengthened and refreshed; and truly, dear sister, I hope in the Lord, through His strength, we shall be clear of all; but our trials are many, especially among false brethren, which as for the particulars at present I shall not commit to paper. Oh! dear sister, if it were not the living power of God, it could never abide all the blows that come against it; but in all this we faint not, but can truly say, our strength is renewed every morning — glory to God on high.

My love is dear to thee, beyond what can be committed to paper, for the truth's sake, and thy care over the flock of God; for which God will thee reward. So, with my dear love to all thy dear children and servants in the truth, I remain

Thy dear brother in the labour of the Gospel,

AMBROSE RIGGE."

In the year 1660, George Fox was apprehended at her house, and committed to Lancaster prison. Gough, the historian, relates, that "Margaret Fell considering the forcible entry and searching of her house, and arresting of her guest there, as a violation of the liberty of the subject, and an injury offered to her, published the following brief narrative of his apprehension:"

"To all magistrates, concerning the wrong taking up and imprisoning George Fox at Lancaster:

I do inform the governors of this nation, that Henry Porter, Mayor of Lancaster, sent a warrant with four constables to my house, for which he had no authority nor order. They searched my house, and apprehended George Fox in it, who was not guilty of the breach of any law, or of any offence against any in the nation. And they had him taken before the said Henry Porter, there was bail offered, what he would demand for his appearance, to answer what could be laid to his charge: but he (contrary to law, if he had taken him lawfully) denied to accept of any bail, and clapt him up in close prison. After he was in prison a copy of the mittimus was demanded, and which ought not to be denied to any prisoner, that so he may see what is laid to his charge; but it was denied him, a copy he could not have, only they were suffered to read it over, and every thing there charged against him was utterly false; he was not guilty of any one charge in it, as will be proved, and manifested to the nation. So let the governors consider it. I am concerned in this thing, inasmuch as he was apprehended in my house; and if he be guilty, I am so too. So I desire to have this searched out.

MARGARET FELL."

She further determined on a journey to London, to solicit the King's protection, and lay the circumstances of George Fox's imprisonment before him.

Her narrative proceeds: "In the year 1660, King Charles the Second came into England, and within two weeks after, I was moved of the Lord to go to London, to speak to the King concerning the truth, and the sufferers for it, for there were then many hundreds of our Friends in prison in the three nations of England, Scotland and Ireland, which were put in by former powers. I spake often to the King, and wrote many papers and letters unto him, and many books were given by our Friends to the Parliament, and great service was done at that time. And they were fully informed of our peaceable principles and practices. I staid in London at that time one year and three months, doing service for the Lord, in visiting Friends' meetings, and giving papers and letters to the King and council, whenever there was occasion. And I wrote and gave papers and letters to every one of the family several times, viz., to the King, to the Dukes of York and Gloucester, and to the Queen mother, to the Princess of Orange, and to the Queen of Bohemia. I was moved of the Lord to visit them all, and to write unto them, and did give them many books and papers, and did lay our principles and doctrines before them, and desired that they let us have discourse with their priests, preachers and teachers, and if they could prove us erroneous, then let them manifest it; but if our principles and doctrines be found according to the doctrine of Christ and the Apostles and saints in primitive times, then let us have our liberty. But we could never get any of them to meet with our Friends. Nevertheless they were very quiet, and we had great liberty, and had our meetings very peaceably for the first half year after the King came in, until the Fifth Monarchy men raised an insurrection and tumult in the city of London, and then all our meetings were disturbed, and Friends taken up; which if they had not been, we were informed the King had intended to have given us liberty. For at that very time, there was an order signed by the King and council for the Quakers' liberty, and just when it should have gone to the press, the Fifth

Monarchy men* arose, and then our Friends were very hardly used, and taken up at their meetings generally, even until many prisons throughout the nation were filled with them. Many a time did I go to the King about them, who promised me always that they should be set at liberty; we had several in the council friendly to us, and we gave many papers to them; and with much ado, and attendance at that time, about a quarter of a year after their first taking Friends to prison, a general proclamation from the King and council was granted, for setting the Quakers at liberty. Then I had freedom in spirit to return home to visit my children and family."

By the solicitations of M. Fell and Anne Curtis (whose father had suffered death for endeavouring to bring in the King), they obtained, at this time, an order for the removal of G. Fox to London; he was brought up by habeas corpus, before

* "Their leader was Thomas Venner, a wine cooper, who, in his little conventicle in Coleman street, warmed his admirers with passionate expectations of a fifth universal monarchy, under the personal reign of *King Jesus* upon earth, and that the saints were to take the kingdom to themselves. To introduce this imaginary kingdom, they marched out of their meeting-house towards St. Paul's churchyard, on Sunday, January 6, 1661, to the number of about fifty men, well armed, with a resolution to subvert the present government, or die in the attempt. This mad insurrection gave the court a handle for breaking through the late declaration of indulgence, within three months after it was published." — *Neale.*

the court of the King's bench; whence the matter was referred to the King and council. No accuser appearing, to criminate him, he was honourably discharged, after an imprisonment of twenty weeks.

In Margaret Fell's letters to King Charles the Second, and the Dukes of York and Gloucester, soon after their return to the kingdom, she "affectionately warns them in the sight of the Lord, the heart-searcher, not to slight the tenders of His love, lest they should be hardened; wishing them to consider the goodness of the Lord in their several preservations, and restoration out of their troubles, into the desired nation, throne and kingdom of their father, and not to take the glory and honour unto themselves; but to let the Lord have the glory thereof, who restored them without the shedding of blood, or loss of lives. Acquainting them, how that God had a suffering people in the nation, which he hath owned, and will own, and reproved and overthrown powers for their sakes whom he has blessed. Signifying, also, that God had brought the King to the throne to try him, what he and they would do for His people, desiring them not to forget His benefits and mercies towards them, and that their hands might be kept out of blood and persecution; for when the innocent were wronged and persecuted, God will plead for and stand by them," &c. Intimating "she was moved of the Lord to write to them beforehand, that they might not be found actors against God and his people; also warning them to take heed whom they let come near them, lest they should be betrayed by dissemblers, or malicious and temporizing spirits who have turned with every power for their own ends."

In her second letter to the King, she desires that he would "Take care for the nation as for his own family, that every one might enjoy his particular right and property, and liberty of conscience; seeing God is delivering His people from under oppressors, that they may serve Him in freeness of spirit who hath heard the cry of the oppressed, and His ears are open to the prayers of the innocent. And that, therefore, it would be good for the King, that his ears should not be shut, lest his heart should grow hard, that he should not slight what they say unto him, who have a testimony for the Lord, and He will bear them witness, when He comes to make inquisition for blood."

In her third letter to the King, delivered by her own hands, on account of his proclamation for bringing to trial those who had been instrumental in the death of his father, she says: "Since God brought him into this nation in love and mercy without shedding of blood, or revengings, she wishes that he would consider this and show mercy; seeing the Lord saith to the merciful, I will show myself merciful, but to the froward I will show myself froward. Advising him not to look out at those that would incense him to revenge, which is not the will of God, nor good for the King, whose best way is to show mercy and forgiveness, and commit his cause to the God of heaven; and let his heart be inclined unto love and mercy, and to grant liberty to the tender consciences of the people; where God's throne is, there no plots, or evil intentions, or secret conspiracies should ever prevail against him," &c. &c.

The following letter she addressed to the King upon the death of the Duke of Gloucester:

"The Lord is come very near thee. Oh! that thou wouldst consider it, and see His hand, that thereby thou mayst learn righteousness, and do justly, love mercy, and walk humbly with the Lord, that so thy throne may be established; and that thou wouldst see the Lord testifying, that He doth not love pride, vanity and vain glory; that now, in the very time of your joy, he hath turned it into mourning. The God of power give you to understand His will and mind, that thou mayst make Him thy joy, who hath the life and breath of all men in His hand."

During her sojourn in London, she paid a visit to Col. Hacker, a day or two before his execution, he being one of the judges of King Charles the First, and now condemned for the part he took in that transaction; he also having been a very violent persecutor of George Fox a few years before. She reminded him of what he had formerly done against the innocent; he remembered it, and said he knew well to whom she alluded, and had trouble on him for it.

It is related of her, that "as a tender mother,

being sensible of the exercise and trial of her dear children, for her long absence from them, and family, she wrote many tender and consolatory letters to them for their encouragement in the truth, and satisfaction in the Lord on her behalf; excusing her long absence, as being so deeply engaged in His fear to clear her conscience, and for His suffering people's sake. Intimating to them how desirable it would be to her to return home to her dear and beloved children, so soon as the Lord pleased to clear her from her long and laborious attending, on behalf of His oppressed people."

The following appears to be one of the letters alluded to:—

"*London*, 25*th of* 8*th mo.* (10*th mo.*) 1660.

My dearly beloved lambs and babes—My love is to you all; and my prayer to the Lord is for you all, that in His arm and power you may be kept in the bosom of His love, there to be nursed and cherished up to eternal life.

G. F. is now freed, blessed be the Lord God—whose arm and power alone hath done it—after he had appeared before the judge who sent for him; then he appeared before the Lord Chief Justice of England in his chamber; and the next day he appeared before them all in open court, in the King's bench; and all this after the King had granted an order to set him free; but they would not set him free till he had appeared in all these places, to see if any thing would come against him. It was of great service for the truth.

I cannot write at present punctually the time of my return, for I do feel that I am not yet clear of this place; but do still wait for the Lord's will and pleasure, and in his time to be manifested to me; and may you rest satisfied in that, for *there* is everlasting peace, and *there* you will enjoy me. I do not know how suddenly the Lord may give me my freedom to come home; but when it is, I shall embrace it lovingly. Let me hear of the little ones, how it is with them all (you mention little of them when you write); and my desire is to hear of you all, and of your well being in the Lord. It may be that you have heard ere this, that James Naylor hath finished his natural life, and hath laid down this body of earth about three-score miles off London.

So no more, but my love in the Lord Jesus is with you; and as soon as the Lord gives me leave, I shall return. The eternal arm of the Almighty be with you. M. F."

"I staid at home about nine months, and then was moved of the Lord to go to London again, not knowing what might be the matter or business that I should go for. At Warrington, I met with an act of Parliament made against the Quakers for refusing oaths. And when I came to London, I heard the King had gone to meet the Queen, and to be married to her at Hampton Court. At this time Friends' meetings at London were much troubled with soldiers, pulling

Friends out of their meetings, and beating them with their muskets and swords; insomuch that several were wounded and bruised by them; and many were cast into prison, through which many lost their lives; and all this being done to a peaceable people, only for worshipping God, as they in conscience were persuaded. Then I saw the King and Duke of York at Hampton Court, and I wrote several letters to them, and therein gave them to understand what desperate and dangerous work there was in London; and how the soldiers came in with lighted matches, and drawn swords among Friends, when they were met in the fear and dread of the Lord to worship Him; and if they would not stop that cruel persecution, it was very like that more innocent blood would be shed, and that would witness against their actions, and lie upon them, and the nation. And within some certain days after, they beat some Friends so cruelly at the Bull and Mouth (meeting) that two died thereof.

The King told me that *his* soldiers did not trouble us, nor should they, and said the city soldiers were not his, and they would do as they pleased with them; and after a little time they were more moderate, and the King promised me that he would set those at liberty that were in prison; and when he brought his Queen to London, he set them at liberty.

And then I came home again, when I had staid about four months in and about London."

The following is the substance of a letter written by her and presented to King Charles the Second at Hampton Court, upon the renewal of the persecution under the law for "The preventing mischiefs and dangers that may arise from certain persons called Quakers, and others, refusing to take lawful oaths:"

'KING CHARLES — Often has the desire of my heart been to God for thee, that thou mightest be preserved out of persecuting the saints and people of God, who hath been gracious and long suffering, whilst moderation hath in some measure been kept to tender consciences; and certainly that promise that thou mad'st in true simplicity, as I do believe, was then in thy heart, that thou wouldst give liberty to tender consciences, I am assured it is upon record in the sight of the Lord God; and thou art bound unto Him in thy conscience to perform. And therefore is my heart affected with the danger that thou incurrest; seeing merciless men are set to work to come into the meetings of God's people, with swords, pistols and muskets, as if it were against thieves or open professed enemies. It is strongly on my heart once more to give thee warning to take care of these things, to take a little view of them betimes before it is too late. You have made an act against us, for what cause the Lord knows, we being harmless and innocent, and tender towards you, although our sufferings have been great; but since you have made a law, it is unreasonable you should exceed it in severity. These things, with many more, are laid upon me from the Lord to lay before thee, who hath put power in thy hand to see righteousness and equity acted in the kingdom; that you may not provoke the Lord is the desire of my heart, who am a true and faithful lover of thy soul."

The following beautiful letter was addressed to her in London by Francis Howgill, who subsequently ended his days in prison, for the testimony of the truth: —

"*Grayrigg*, 29*th of* 7*th mo.* (9*th mo.*), 1661.

DEAR MARGARET —

In Him, who has become a place of broad rivers and streams unto us, and the portion of our cup, and the lot of our inheritance, do I most dearly salute thee.

The former days are not forgotten by me, nor the years past, when we were all made to drink of one cup, and were baptized into the death and suffering of Christ: and were made to drink it willingly, knowing it was our portion allotted unto us of the Lord, which we could not pass, but must drink thereof. And though it was irksome and grievous unto us, when our strength was but small, yet God, out of His infinite love and mercy, strengthened us to bear, and to suffer, and to deny that which hid immortality and life from us. And He bore us up in His arms, and made us to endure with patience the sufferings and the death; that so we might obtain the resurrection of the dead: which indeed was a blessed time; though for a moment it seemed grievous. But now, having obtained the resurrection of the dead, being baptized into the resurrection and into the life, more blessedness is known, even spiritual blessings, which God hath given us to enjoy in heavenly places in Christ Jesus: that like as we suffered one for another, and one with another, so we might be made to rejoice one with another, and for another, and in Him alone; in whom all our fresh springs are, and from whom our joy and gladness and consolation spring. He hath opened the springs of the great deep, and hath made life spring up, whereby His little ones are refreshed, and the young men strengthened, and the ancient and honourable confirmed and established. Holy and revered be His name forevermore, who is exalting His glorious mountain above the top of all the earth; and making Jerusalem the praise and glory and admiration of the whole earth. And let me tell thee, I am no more weary than the first day the sickle was put into the harvest; when we went out sowing the seed weeping and in tears: but seeing sheaves brought home, and full loads into the barn, and full draughts caught in the net, it hath made me look beyond fainting—blessed be the Lord.

I am glad thou stayest so long in that city (London), in which we have had many a burden and weary day: but that fruit is brought forth unto God, plenteously countervails all, and makes me forget travail. I have been northward in Northumberland, Bishoprick, and upon the east sea, and back to York: truly the garden for the most part is very pleasant, and gives a goodly smell, now when the south wind blows upon it.

Dearly farewell in the holy covenant of life,

FRANCIS HOWGILL."

CHAPTER III. 1662–1668.

PERFORMS A RELIGIOUS VISIT IN SEVERAL COUNTIES — MEETS WITH GEORGE FOX — THEIR ARREST AND IMPRISONMENT IN LANCASTER CASTLE — HER TRIAL — TESTIMONY AGAINST SWEARING — PREMUNIRED, AND REMANDED TO PRISON — LETTER FROM HER DAUGHTER—LETTER TO HER SON-IN-LAW AND WIFE—INEFFECTUAL EFFORTS TO OBTAIN HER RELEASE — THE HARDSHIPS AND PRIVATIONS OF HER IMPRISONMENT — EXPOSTULATORY LETTER TO THE KING—DESCRIPTION OF LANCASTER CASTLE — HER RELEASE.

In the year 1663, in company with one of her daughters, she performed a religious journey of about one thousand miles, visiting Friends in Somersetshire, Devonshire and Dorsetshire to Bristol, from thence to Yorkshire, into Northumberland and Westmoreland. In the course of their travels they met with George Fox, who accompanied them home, soon after which he was arrested and committed to Lancaster castle.

She says: "About a month after the same justices sent for me to Ulverston, and when I came there they asked me several questions, and seemed to be offended at me for keeping a meeting at my house, and said they would tender me the oath of allegiance. I answered they *knew* I could not swear, and why should they send for me from my own house, where I was about my lawful occasions, to ensnare me? What had I done? They said if I would not keep meetings at my house, they would not tender me the oath. I told them I should not deny my faith and principles for any thing they could do unto me; and whilst it pleased the Lord to let me have a house, I would endeavour to worship him in it. So they caused the oath to be read, and tendered it unto me; and I refused it, telling them, I could not take any oath for conscience' sake, Christ Jesus having forbid it. They then made a mittimus and committed me prisoner to Lancaster Castle, and there George Fox and I remained in prison until the next assizes; and then they indicted us upon the statute for denying the oath of allegiance; for they tendered it to us both again at the assizes; but they said to me, if I would not keep a meeting at my house, I should be set at liberty. But I answered the judge that I rather chose a prison for obeying God, than my liberty for obeying men contrary to my conscience. So we were called several times before them at that assizes, and the indictments were found against us. The next assizes we came to trial, and George Fox's indictment was found to be dated wrong, both in the day of the month, and in the year of the King's reign, so that it was quashed; but mine they would not allow the errors that were found in it to make it void, although there were several; so they passed the sentence of premunire upon me, which was, that I should be out of the King's protection, and forfeit all my estate, real and personal, to the King, and be imprisoned for life. But the great God of heaven and earth so supported my spirit under this severe sentence, that I was not terrified, but gave this answer to Judge Turner, who gave this sentence, *Although I am out of the King's protection, yet I am not out of the protection of the Almighty God:* so there I remained in prison twenty months, before I could get so much favour of the sheriff, as to go to my own house; which then I did for a little time, and returned to prison again."

Whilst before the judges, she bore this clear and noble testimony against swearing, and vindicated herself from all cause of offence:—

"I am here this day upon the account of my conscience, and not for any evil, or wrong done to any man, but for obeying Christ's doctrine and commands, who hath said in the Scriptures: 'That God is a spirit, and that His worship is in spirit and truth:' and for keeping meetings in the unity of this spirit. Now you profess yourselves to be Christians, and you own the Scriptures to be true; and for the obedience of the plain words of Scripture, and for the testimony of my conscience, am I here.

I say this to the oath, as I have said in this place before now, Christ Jesus has commanded me not to swear at all; and that is the only cause and no other; the righteous Judge of heaven and earth knows, before whose throne of justice you must all appear one day; and His eye sees us all, and beholds us at this present time, and hears and sees all our words and actions: and therefore every one ought to be serious; for the place of judgment is weighty. And this I do testify to you here, where the Lord's eye beholds us all, that for the matter or substance of the oath, and the end for which it was intended, I do own one part and deny the other. That is to say, I do own truth, and faithfulness, and obedience to the King, in all his just and lawful demands and commands. I do also deny all plottings and contrivings against the King, and all Popish supremacy, and conspiracy: and I can no more transgress against King Charles in these things, than I can disobey Christ Jesus' commands. And by the same power, and by virtue of the same word, which has commanded not to swear at all, the same doth bind me in my conscience, that I can neither plot nor contrive against the King, nor do him nor any man upon the earth any wrong; and I do not deny this oath only, because it is the oath of allegiance; but I deny it, because it is an oath, and because Christ Jesus has said, *Swear not at all, neither by heaven, nor by earth, nor any other oath;* and if I might gain the whole world for swearing of an oath, I could not; and whatever I have to lose this day, for not swearing, I am ready to offer up."

One of the justices observed: "Mrs. Fell, you may with a good conscience put in security to have no more meetings at your house, if you *cannot* take the oath."

"Wilt thou make it good," said she, "that I may with a safe conscience make an engagement to forbear meetings, for fear of losing my liberty and estate? Wilt not thou and all here judge me, that it was for saving my estate and liberty that I did it? And should I not, in this, deny my testimony; and would not this defile my conscience?"

Considerable effort was made by some of her friends in London to prevent the sentence of premunire being passed upon her, and some of her children applied to the King in her behalf; but without any effect. The following is a letter from one of her daughters on the subject:—

"*Mile End Green, near London,*
27*th* 4*th mo.*, 1664.

ENDEARED AND TENDER-HEARTED MOTHER:—

My duty and very dear love is freely given and remembered unto thee, as also my very dear love is to dear George Fox. This is chiefly to let thee understand that yesterday sister and I went to White Hall; where we spoke to the King, and told him if he would please to signify something to the judges, before they went their circuit, to release you; otherwise it would be past, for the time drew very near of the assizes. He said he would release you, if we would promise you would not go to meetings. Sister said we could make no such engagement; for the meeting had been kept many years, and never had done any harm. He said, cannot your mother keep within her own family, as she may have five persons present, but she must have such tumultuous meetings? We said she hath no such meetings, they are only her neighbors that come. The King said there were some Quakers in the last plot. Sister said that could not be proved. He said he had letters about it, and their names. So Chifines* bid us come on the fourth day; and we intend to go to-morrow. I was there about a week since, and told the King, that now the assizes drew very near, if he did not do something for thee, they would run thee into a premunire, and get thy estate from thee and thy children; and I desired him to take it into consideration. He was then very loving to me, and said he would take it into consideration; and he said, 'they shall not have her estate from her:' he took me by the hand as soon as he came near me. I also spoke to Prince Rupert, and desired him to put the King in mind of it: and he said he would do what he could in it; and went then to the King and spoke to him. Prince Rupert hath always been very loving to Friends; and hath often spoken to the King about you.

Sister gives the renewed remembrance of her entire love to thee and dear G. F., as also doth my brother; I suppose sisters Isabel and Sarah will be gone: remember me to sisters Susanna and Rachel.

I am thy dutiful and obedient daughter,

MARY FELL."

The following letter, written by M. Fell, when in prison, to her son-in-law, John Rouse, and his wife,

---

* One of the pages.

after she had been premunired, shows, that having been deeply taught in the school of Christ, and strengthened by Him, she had learned, like the Apostle Paul, that in whatsoever state she found herself, therewith to be content:—

"*Lancaster Castle*, 1*st* 8*th mo.* (10*th mo.*), 1664.

"As I have often said to thee, give up to be crossed; *that* is the way to please the Lord, and to follow Him in His own will and way, whose way is the best. Let nothing enter thy mind concerning anything about me, for I am well contented in the work of the Lord. I know your care and tenderness were not wanting to Friends; and so be all satisfied in the will of the Lord God. I hope in the Lord that you are all together, ere this come to you. Be all satisfied and content with the will of the Lord; and let neither murmuring nor repining enter any of your minds; and let not sorrow fill your hearts, for we have all cause to rejoice in the Lord evermore, and I most of all.

Colonel Kirby causes our bonds to be renewed and straightened more and more: and they lock up G. F. under pretence of an order that should come from London. Get this enclosed letter of G. F.'s sent to Gilbert Latey, that G. Whitehead and they may draw out what they see convenient.

MARGARET FELL."

Some attempts were afterwards made to obtain her release, or at least some mitigation of the rigours of her imprisonment, but with no better success. Gilberty Latey, in one of his letters, giving an account of an interview he had with Lord D'Aubigny on her behalf, says: "That neither the King nor chancellor would do anything at all for us. Neither could any man be heard to speak for us. Then I told him of the unjustness of thy imprisonment, and of the badness of the jury, and its being contrary to law, and that thou desired nothing but a fair prison, and that the thieves and murderers had more liberty than thee, and that thou wast locked up in a bad room, and Friends not suffered to come to speak to thee; and I told him I had a paper of it, and desired that he would hand it. He told me he was sorry with all his heart, but he would tell me no lie; he was sure nothing could be done, and he believed they did it on purpose to vex us; and so I parted with him; for he said he could do nothing, for all the clergy were against us, and nothing could be done at all, neither did he care to meddle with the paper at all; so I was fain to leave him."

Gough, the historian, remarks: "Such rigorous imprisonment as these people, particularly George Fox and Margaret Fell, were subject to, being in smoky rooms, in such bad condition that the rain came in upon them in abundance, was more than sufficient punishment for petty criminals, and an evidence of the unfeeling malice of their persecutors needlessly to expose Margaret Fell in particular to such hardships, a woman of estate, the widow of a judge, and a man of consequence in the country, who had been used to comfortable accommodations in her own house, and was every way on a level with her persecutors, except the possession of power. But all the hardships she suffered, in being arbitrarily forced from her home and family, without cause or crimination, and hurried to this dismal jail, was not a sufficient gratification of the groundless enmity of these magistrates, until they went the furthest lengths they could go, by prosecuting her to a premunire, realizing the proverb, *summum jus, summa injuria: the execution of perverted law is accumulated injury.*"

She earnestly expostulated with the King, on the injustice of the law authorizing the banishment of Friends, reminding him of her former interview with him, and the rigours of her own imprisonment, in a letter addressed to him "from my prison at Lancaster Castle, the 6th day of the 6th month, 1666," some extracts from which are here inserted:

"King Charles:—

I desire thee to read this over, which may be for thy satisfaction and profit.

In the fear of the Lord God stand still, and consider what thou and you have been doing these six years, since the Lord brought you peaceably into this realm, and made you rulers over this people. The righteous eye of the Almighty hath been over you, and hath seen all your doings and actions.

What laws have you made or changed, save such as have laid oppression and bondage on the consciences of God's people, and that of no less penalty than *banishment out of their native country?* The greatest crime that you could find with the people of God was, that they obeyed and worshipped Christ Jesus: so that the greatest stroke that hath appeared of your justice hath been upon such as you counted offenders for worshipping of God, insomuch that several of your judges of the land have several times said, in open court, to any that did confess they met to worship the Lord God, that that was crime enough, whereby they could proceed to banishment. And when it was asked in open court, whether it was now become a transgression or a crime in England to worship God? He that was then Chief Justice of England answered: 'Yes, yes.' Oh! wonderful, let this be chronicled in England for after ages, that all magistrates may dread and fear so to affront the Almighty; except they dare say they are stronger than he.

And all this hath been without any just cause given at any time by that people, which was the object of this law; so that men, that had but the least measure of righteousness and equity, could never have proceeded on to have inflicted such a height of punishment, without some just ground.

And all that was ever pretended, was but suspicion, which can never be paralleled; to be prosecuted to such a height of suffering without a just ground given, although occasion hath been continually sought and watched for, but never found; but the Lord has preserved His people innocent and harmless; and therefore is He engaged to plead their cause, into whose hand it is wholly given and committed.

I desire you also to consider seriously, in the fear of the Lord, what effects and fruits these things have brought forth.

I believe it hath brought hundreds of God's people to their graves; it hath also rendered this realm, and the governors of it, cruel, in the eyes of all people, both within its own body, and in other nations; besides the guilt of innocent blood lies upon this kingdom.

Since which time, the Lord in His judgment hath taken many thousands of its people away by His two judgments, pestilence and sword.

And before any of this was, when you first entered into this kingdom, I was sent of the Lord to you, to inform you truly of the state and condition of our people; and when I came before thee, O King, I told thee I was come to thee on behalf of an innocent, harmless, peaceable people; which words I would then, and ever since, and should at this day seal with my blood, if I were put to it. And thy answer was to me, *if they be peaceable they shall be protected.*

I also wrote to thee several times concerning our faith and principles, how that we could not swear for conscience' sake; neither could we take up arms, nor plot, nor contrive to do any man wrong nor injury, much less the King. I also told you, that we must worship God, for God required it of us.

We did likewise give you many of our books,

which contained our faith, and principles and doctrine, that thereby we might be tried by the Scriptures of Truth (which all of you do profess), whether our principles were erroneous or no; and to that purpose we gave our books to the King and Parliament, and to the bishops and ministers, both ecclesiastical and civil. All this, with much more, I wrote to thee, and warned thee of (I can truly say in the fear of the Lord), in much love and tenderness to thee. And now I may say unto thee, for which of these things hast thou kept me in prison three long winters, in a place not fit for people to lie in; sometimes for wind, and storm, and rain, and sometimes for smoke; so that it is much that I am alive, but that the power and goodness of God hath been with me. I was kept a year and seven months in this prison, before I was suffered to see the house that was mine, or children or family, except they came to me over two dangerous sands in the cold winter, when they came with much danger of their lives; but since the last assizes I have had a little more respect from this sheriff, than formerly from others. And in all this I am very well satisfied; and praise the Lord, who counts me worthy to suffer for His sake.

And now after all my sufferings, in the same love that I visited thee in the beginning, I desire thee once more to fear the Lord God, *by whom Kings rule, and Princes decree justice; who sets up one, and pulls down another, at His pleasure.*

And let not the guilt of the burthen of the breach of that word that passed from thee at Breda, lie upon thy conscience, but as thou promised when thou wast in distress, and also renewed it many times since, that thou wouldst give liberty to tender consciences; in the fear of the Lord perform it, and purge thy conscience of it; and hearken not to wicked counsellors, that have stopped it in thee all this time; for they will bear none of thy burden for thee, when the Lord pleads for breach of covenant with Him and His people; I know it hath been often in thy heart to perform it, and thou hast seen what fruit the want of it hath brought forth. So if thou lovest thy eternal peace and comfort with the Lord, try what the performance of it will bring forth, thou wilt thereby see thou hast hearkened to wrong counsellors. And every mortal man hath but a moment in this life, either to serve, fear and honour the Lord, and therein to receive mercy from Him; or else to transgress, sin, disobey, and dishonour Him, and receive the judgment of eternal misery.

So none of you know how long, or how short your day may be; therefore fear not man, that can kill the body; but fear the Lord, who, when he hath killed the body, can cast the soul and body into hell; yea, I say unto you fear Him.

From a true lover of all your souls (though a sufferer by you), and the desire of my heart is, that you may take these things into consideration betime, before it be too late, and set open the prison doors, and let the innocent go free, and that will take part of the burden and guilt off you, lest the door of mercy be shut against you."

Lancaster Castle, the prison of Margaret Fell, in its present form, was founded by John of Gaunt, Duke of Lancaster, in the 14th century. This castle and its predecessor have been noted strongholds, famous in British history from the time of the Romans to the days of Cromwell and the Pretender. A recent writer thus describes the castle, and the room occupied by George Fox: "He who penetrates within the enclosure of the castle will wonder at the kind of life which kings and princes must have led in the days of its erection. Here are the same rooms of John of Gaunt, visited sometimes by his father, Edward the Third — small, stately, strong apartments, having few windows in the exterior, and these narrowed to the smallest possible dimensions — well fitted to serve as the prisons they have since become. Fox's room was in the donjon, and the window of what was his residence during many long, dreary months is conspicuous over the greater part of the ancient town. It was evidently, at one period, a room of considerable size, but in Fox's day it was old and ruinous. He could scarcely walk across his apartment, because of the dilapidated state of the floor. The smoke that came from the other prisons was so dense, that sometimes a burning candle was scarcely visible, and he was in imminent danger of being choked; and the turnkey was with difficulty persuaded to unlock one of the upper doors, in order to let out the smoke. In wet weather it rained upon his bed. The inconveniences of his prison affected Fox to such a degree, during a cold and prolonged winter, that his body became swollen, and his limbs benumbed. When he was brought up at the March assizes, 1665, he was so weak that he could scarcely stand or move."

"Nor were Fox's friends in this neighbourhood allowed to escape. Many of his followers, and amongst them Margaret Fell, at whose house he had been apprehended, were also confined in the castle, where an apartment exists, still called the *Quaker's room*, because it was the scene of the sufferings of many of these oppressed and unresisting Christians." *

Having endured an imprisonment of about four years, M. Fell was at length set at liberty by an order of the King and council, in the year 1668.

* At one time there were 4500 Friends in prison in England and Wales. In 1662, 20 died in different prisons in London, and 7 more after their liberation, from ill treatment. In 1664, 25 died; and in 1665, 52 more. The number that perished in this way throughout the whole kingdom amounted to 369. For a full account of the cruelties practised against the early Friends, the reader is referred to two folio volumes entitled "*Besse's Sufferings.*"

CHAPTER IV. 1668–1690.

VISITS IMPRISONED FRIENDS — HER MARRIAGE WITH GEORGE FOX AT BRISTOL — AGAIN IMPRISONED ON THE OLD PREMUNIRE — HER HUSBAND AND TWO OF HER CHILDREN OBTAIN AN ORDER FOR HER DISCHARGE — WHICH IS DISREGARDED —SHE OBTAINS A FREE DISCHARGE UNDER THE GREAT SEAL, RELEASING HER AND HER ESTATE FROM THE PREMUNIRE — VISITS LONDON TO TAKE LEAVE OF HER HUSBAND, WHO GOES TO AMERICA — HIS RETURN, AND IMPRISONMENT IN WORCESTER JAIL — HE IS PREMUNIRED — HER EFFORTS IN HIS BEHALF — HIS RELEASE, AND RETURN TO SWARTHMORE — LETTER TO THOMAS LOWER — RETURNS TO LONDON—VISITS THE KING — HIS DEATH — INTERVIEW WITH KING JAMES— FRESH IMPRISONMENT — EPISTLE TO WOMEN FRIENDS OF LONDON.

Shortly after her release, "she was moved of the Lord" to make an extended journey through many of the counties of England, visiting most of the Friends that were imprisoned in the nation, and spending a number of weeks in London and Bristol.

It was on her return from this visit that she again met with George Fox, and remarks:

"It was eleven years after my former husband's decease; and G. Fox being then returned from visiting Friends in Ireland; at Bristol he declared his intentions of marriage with me; and there was also our marriage solemnized, in a public meeting of many Friends, who were our witnesses."

George Fox, in his journal, gives the following relation of his marriage. Before proceeding therein he was careful that the rights of her children should not suffer, and had their free consent, for, said he, "I would have all things done plainly, for I sought not any advantage to myself." *

"I had seen from the Lord a considerable time before, that I should take Margaret Fell to be my wife; and when I first mentioned it to her, she felt the answer of life from God thereunto. But though the Lord had opened this thing to me, yet I had not received a command from Him for the accomplishing of it then. Wherefore I let the thing rest, and went on in the work and service of the Lord, according as he led me; travelling in this nation and Ireland. But now being at Bristol, and finding Margaret Fell there, it opened in me from the Lord that the thing should be accomplished. And so our intention of marriage was laid before Friends, both privately and

---

* In confirmation of this, and showing the justice and conscientiousness that characterized George Fox, in regard to property, and of his opinions being in advance of those then prevailing on the subject, the following circumstance, related in his journal, will serve to illustrate. Being prosecuted for tithes against his wife's estate at Swarthmore, he and William Mead, her son-in-law, appeared before the court, "when," he says, "William Mead told the judges that I had engaged never to meddle with my wife's estate. The judges would hardly believe that any man would do so; whereupon he showed them the writing under my hand and seal; at which they wondered." — *Fox's Journal*, vol. ii. p. 302.

publicly, to their full satisfaction, many of whom gave testimony that it was of God. Afterwards a meeting being appointed on purpose for the accomplishing thereof, in the public meeting-house at Broad Mead, in Bristol, we took each other in marriage; and the Lord joined us together in honourable marriage, in the everlasting covenant and immortal Seed of life."*

---

* The following is a copy of her marriage certificate: —

"These are to signify unto all whom this may concern that on the eighteenth day of the eighth month in the year one thousand, six hundred sixty nine, George Fox and Margarett ffell propounded their intentions of joininge together in the honourable marriage, in the covenant of God in Mens meetinge, at Broadmead, within the Citty of Bristoll (having before made mention of such their intentions to several ffriends,) on the behalf of which there were several testimonies given, both by the children and relations of the said Margarett, then present, and several others, in the power of the Lord, both of men and women, declaring their satisfaction, and approbation of their declared intention of marriage. And likewise at another meetinge both of men and women, at the place aforesaide, on the twenty first day of the month and year aforesaide, the said George Fox and Margarett ffell did againe publish their intention of joininge together in the honourable marriage in the covenant of God, unto which, there were againe many livinge testimonies borne by the relations and ffriends then present, both of Men and Women. And the same intentions of Marriage beinge againe published by Dennis Hollister at our public meetinge-place aforesaide, on the two and twentyeth day of the month and year aforesaide, and then againe, a public testimony was given to the same, that it was of God who had brought it to passe.

Her narrative proceeds: "Soon after I came home, there came another order to cast me into prison again; and the sheriff of Lancashire sent his bailiff, and pulled me out of my own house, and had me to prison at Lancaster Castle, where I continued a whole year; and most of that time I was sick and weakly. And after some time my husband endeavoured to get

---

And for the full accomplishment of the aforesaide proposal, and approved intention, at a publicke meetinge both of men and women ffriends, appointed on purpose for the same thinge, at the place aforesaide, and on the twenty seventh day of the month and year aforesaide, according to the law and ordinance of God, and the example and good order of His people, mentioned in the Scriptures of Truth, who tooke each other before witnesses, and the Elders of the people, as Laban appointed a meetinge, at the marriage of Jacob, and as a meetinge was appointed on purpose, when Boaz and Ruth tooke each other, and also as it was in Canaan, where Christ and his disciples went to a marriage. The saide George Fox did solemnly, in the presence of God, and us his people, declare that he tooke the saide Margarett ffell in the everlasting power and covenent of God which is from everlasting to everlasting, and in the honourable marriage, to be his bride, and his wife. And likewise the saide Margarett did solemnly declare that, in the everlastinge power of the mighty God, and in the unalterable word, and in the presence of God, His Angells and his holy assembly, she tooke the saide George Fox to be her husband, unto which marriage, many livinge testimonies were borne in the sence of the power and presence of the livinge God, manifested in the said assembly; of which, we, whose names are here subscribed are witnesses.

Signed by 92 men and women Friends." — *Friends' Review*, vol. i. p. 270.

me out of prison; and a discharge at last was got, under the great seal, and I was set at liberty."

This imprisonment was upon the old premunire, from which she had been discharged the year before. As soon as George Fox reached London after hearing of her fresh incarceration, he sent Mary Lower and Sarah Fell (her children) to the King, to strive to obtain an order for her discharge, which with some difficulty was procured. They carried it to Lancaster, together with the following letter from G. Fox:—

"MY DEAR HEART IN THE TRUTH AND LIFE, THAT CHANGETH NOT:—

It was upon me that Mary Lower and Sarah should go to the King concerning thy imprisonment; and to Kirby, that the power of the Lord might appear over them all in thy deliverance. They went; and then they thought to have come down; but it was upon me to stay them a little longer, that they might follow the business till it was effected, which it now is and is here sent. The late declaration of mine has been very serviceable, people being generally satisfied with it.

So no more but my love in the Holy Seed,

GEORGE FOX."

This second intimation of the King's will and pleasure respecting her, was presented to the sheriff by her two daughters; but her old enemies found

5*

means, by some informality in the document, to evade even this command.

Her husband therefore renewed his solicitations for her release; which was at length effected by means of Martha Fisher and another female Friend, who obtained a second interview with the King, and informed him of all their difficulties. The King then granted a free discharge under the great seal, and released both her, and her estate from the penalties of the sentence of premunire, under which she had been suffering for more than five years.

The condescending interference of King Charles, in behalf of Margaret Fox shows, that he was averse to these violent measures against his peaceable non-conforming subjects, and that he would probably have adhered to his proclamation from Breda, promising religious toleration, had he not been driven by his necessities, and extravagance, to concede these arbitrary measures to the high church party, for the sake of obtaining supplies.

She went up to London soon after, to take leave of her husband, then about embarking for America. He was absent two years; she again met him, on his return, at Bristol, whence they proceeded to London, and staid there some time, when they took leave of their friends, and proceeded homewards, in company with her daughter Rachel, stopping at Rickmansworth, on a visit to William Penn and his family, where they were joined by her son-in-law, Thomas Lower. Upon leaving Rickmansworth, they continued their journey through Oxfordshire, visiting

Friends' meetings as they proceeded, and at Tredington, in Worcestshire, they attended a meeting of about two hundred persons, held in a barn; the meeting having quietly dispersed, and they having retired into the house of John Halford, George Fox and Thomas Lower were arrested and committed to Worcester jail: G. Fox being afterwards premunired by the court there, and continued in confinement, she went to him, and had a conference with the judges, and also with the King, endeavouring to obtain his release. The case was subsequently removed by habeas corpus to the King's bench bar, where Judge Hale pronounced the indictment illegal and void, and he was discharged. They returned together to Swarthmore, he being much weakened in body, his health having suffered severely in consequence of his long imprisonment. He continued at home about one and twenty months, before he was sufficiently recovered to resume his travels, being the longest period he remained with his wife since their marriage.

Persecution and distraints still continued, whereby Friends were much distressed and impoverished. She says, in speaking of the difficulties they encountered in these respects: —

"When my husband was at London, it being a time of great persecution by informers, the justices of our country were very severe, and much bent against me, because I kept a meeting at Swarthmore Hall; so they did not fine the house as his, he being absent, but as mine; and fined me £20 for the house, and £20 for speaking in the meeting; and the second time £40 for speaking; and also other Friends for speaking, £20 for the first, and £40 for the second time: those that were not able, they fined others for them, and made great spoil among Friends, by distraining their goods, sometimes for less than half the value; they took thirty head of cattle from me. Their intentions were to ruin and weary us out, and enrich themselves; but the Lord prevented them."

Her son-in-law, Thomas Lower, being premunired and imprisoned, she wrote him the subjoined comforting letter. He was "a physician of London," says Besse, "and visiting George Fox when he was imprisoned in Cornwall, asked him many questions concerning religion, and received such clear answers from G. Fox, that he said 'his words were as a flash of lightning, they ran so through him,' adding, 'he had never met with a man of such wisdom and penetration in his life.' By these means he became fully convinced of the doctrine of truth, which he afterwards made a public profession of." He subsequently married Mary Fell.

"To Thomas Lower and his fellow-sufferers for the testimony of Jesus, when they were premunired, and prisoners in Lauceston Jail: —

Dear Son Lower: —

In the dear and precious blessed unity of the eternal Spirit, and fellowship of the gospel of peace, in this is my heart and soul's love remembered unto thee, and to all thy dear brethren and fellow-prisoners with thee, that suffer for the testimony of Jesus; my soul's desire is to the powerful God for you all, that you may be more than conquerors in Christ Jesus, who is the great King, and Lord over all, and hath all power in heaven and earth in His hands, and all the inhabitants of the earth are but as grasshoppers before Him; and therefore with hearts and courage may His servants and children suffer for Him, without fear or fainting, under those that have but power over the outward man. The Lord preserve you in the dominion over them all; and I am glad to hear in every letter that comes from thee, that ye are well satisfied and content. And I know certainly, the Lord will never be wanting to you, as ye keep faithful and true, and single-hearted to Him; His eye beholds and sees all that His and your enemies can do unto you, and a just and righteous reward from Him they will surely receive.

And my dear love is unto thee, in that which never changes, which gives peace, and content, and faith to look over that which changes.

Thy dear mother in the Lord,

M. Fox.

Swarthmore, 28th of 7th mo., 1683."

"I was moved of the Lord to go to London, in the seventieth year of my age; and the word was in me, that as I had gone to King Charles, when he first came into England, so I should go, and bear to him my last testimony, and let him know how they did abuse us, to enrich themselves: a paper was drawn up, to give a true and certain account how they dealt with me, and other Friends. It was upon my mind, to go first unto the Duke of York; and I wrote a short paper to him, to acquaint him, that as he had sometimes formerly spoke in my behalf to the King, my request was, that he would now do the like for me, or words to that effect. I went with this paper to James' house; and after long waiting, I got to speak to him. But some let him know, that it was I that had been with him and his brother, soon after they came into England. I gave him my little paper, and asked him if he did not remember me? He said, *I do remember you.* Then I desired him to speak to the King for us, for we were under great sufferings, and our persecutors were so severe, that it looked as if they intended to make a prey upon us; he said he could not help, but he would speak to the King. The next day, with much ado, I got to the King, and had my great paper, which was the relation of our sufferings, to present to him; but he was so rough and angry, that he would not take it; but I gave several copies to his nobles. Afterwards I went to Judge Jeffreys, and told him of our sufferings; for he had been in the North country with us, a little before, and he told me we might speak to the King. I answered it was very hard to get to the King; he said, 'give me a paper, and I will speak to him;' but said, 'your papers are too long, give me a short one, and I will speak to him:' so I wrote a little paper from myself, to this effect:—

KING CHARLES:—Thou and thy magistrates put very great and cruel sufferings upon us; but this I must say unto thee, if you make our sufferings to death itself, we shall not, nor dare not, but confess Christ Jesus before men, lest He should deny us before His Father which is in heaven."

"There were some more words, but this was the substance: Jeffreys read it, and said he would give it him; we gave papers to several of those that waited on him, and they gave us some encouragement, that we should be helped; so we expected and waited for it. About a week or two after, in the beginning of the 12th month, George Whitehead and I were going to one of the lords, who had promised George that he would speak to the King for us: we went to his lodgings early in the morning, thinking to speak with him before he went out; but his servants told us he was not within, being gone to the King, who was not well. Then we came forth into Whitehall court; but all the gates were shut, that we could not get forth. So we waited, and walked up and down; and several came from the King, and said, *he could not stand;* others said, *he could not speak.* Then, after some hours waiting, we got through Scotland-yard, and came away; the King continued sick until the sixth day after, and then he died. So this confirmed that word which God put into my heart, *that I was sent to bear my last testimony to the King.*"

"Then James, Duke of York, was proclaimed

King, and about two weeks after, I went to him, and gave him a paper to this effect: —

King James — I have waited here some months, until this change is come, and now I would return home; but I cannot live peaceably there, except I have a word from thee, to give a check to my persecutors.

I spoke to him to the same purpose. He said unto me, *go home, go home.* So after a few weeks I went home.

And a little while after, William Kirby, a justice, one of our greatest persecutors, met with my son-in-law, Daniel Abraham, upon the road, and said to him, tell your mother that now the government will be settled again, and if you keep meetings, you must expect the same again. My son answered him, we must keep meetings, unless you take our lives. Then William Kirby said, we will not take your lives, but whilst you have anything, we will take it. So I wrote a letter to King James, in which I said, Thou bids't me come home, and so I am; but as I said to thee, I could not live peaceably, so it is like to be; and then I hinted in my letter W. Kirby's discourse with my son. And I desired of the King, to let me have something from him, that I might live peaceably at my house.

This letter was delivered to him, and as I heard, he carried it to the council, and it was read; and some of the council said, she desires a protection, that she may live peaceably at her own house; and that some made answer, they could give no protection to an individual: however, I do suppose they gave our persecutors a private caution, for they troubled us no more; but, if that had not been, it is likely they had a mind to begin anew upon us; for a little before the time of the informers, they brought that law upon us, concerning twelve pence a Sunday, so called; and they carried me, and my son and daughter Abraham, to Lancaster prison, and kept us there about three weeks. And when they considered, that they could not fine me, nor my house, when I was in prison, then they let us go home, and soon after they did fine us both for the house, and for speaking as before hinted.

And thus have they troubled and persecuted us divers ways; but the Lord God Almighty hath preserved me, and us, until this day; glorious praises be given to him forevermore.

And the Lord hath given me such strength and ability, that I have been at London, to see my dear husband and children and relatives and friends there in 1690, being the seventy-sixth year of my age; and I was very well satisfied, refreshed and comforted in my journey, and found Friends in much love, praises be returned to the unchangeable God forever. This being nine times that I have been to London, upon the Lord's and His truth's account."

The company of her two daughters, the wives of John Rouse and William Mead, the former residing at Kingston on Thames, and the latter at Goose's in Essex, while on her visits to London, was doubtless very comforting to her, and a great satisfaction to them. These were also favorite resorts of G. Fox when in that neighbourhood.

After returning to her home, she wrote the following epistle to the Women's Meeting in London: —

"Dear Sisters: —

In the eternal blessed truth, into which we are begotten, and in which we stand, and are preserved, as we keep in it, and are guided by it: in this is my dear and unchangeable love remembered unto you all; acknowledging your dear and tender love, when I was with you, in which my heart was rejoiced, to feel the ancient love and unity of the eternal spirit amongst you; and my soul was and is refreshed in my journey, in visiting my dear husband and children, and you my dear Friends. And now I am returned to my own house and family, where I find all well; praised and honoured be my Heavenly Father.

And dear Friends our engagements are great unto the Lord, and he is dear and faithful unto us; and blessed and happy are all they that are dear and faithful unto Him. And those that keep single and chaste unto Him need not fear evil tidings, nor what man can do, for He that hath all power in heaven and earth in His hand, will surely keep His own church and family, those that worship Him, within the measuring line, that measures the temple, and the altar, and those that worship therein, they are kept safe, as in the hollow of His hand.

And so, dear Friends, my heart and soul was so much comforted and refreshed, amongst you, that I could not but signify the remembrance of my dear love unto you; and also my acknowledgment of your dear love and tenderness to my dear husband; for which I doubt not, but the Lord doth and will reward you; into whose hand and arm and power I commit you.

M. Fox.

Swarthmore, 10th of 5th month, 1690."

CHAPTER V. 1690–1702.

DEATH OF GEORGE FOX — AGAIN GOES TO LONDON — ADDRESS TO KING WILLIAM — HER DEATH, AND DYING SAYINGS — TESTIMONY OF HER CHILDREN, AND OTHER FRIENDS, TO HER CHARACTER — BURIED AT SWARTHMORE.

In the latter part of the year 1690, her husband, who had been in a declining state of health for several years previous, died at the house of Henry Gouldney, in London, after a few days' sickness, in much contentment and peace. "It fell to the lot of William Penn," says Clarkson, "to communicate this event to his wife." "I am to be," says he, "the teller to thee of sorrowful tidings, in some respects, which is this, that thy dear husband, and my beloved and dear friend, finished his glorious testimony this night about half an hour after nine, being sensible to the last breath. Oh! he is gone, and left us in the storm that is over our heads, surely in great mercy to him, but as an evidence to us of sorrow to come: a prince, indeed, is fallen in Israel to-day; he died as he lived, a lamb, minding the things of God and His church to the last, in an universal spirit."

They had been married about twenty-one years, and during that period he had passed but a small part of the time with her, his various religious engagements keeping him almost constantly away from Swarthmore.

This circumstance probably gave rise to some censorious remarks, for his wife, in speaking of it, says: "And though the Lord had provided him with an outward habitation, he was not willing to stay in it, because it was so remote and far from London, where his service mostly lay. And my concern for God and His holy and eternal truth was then in the north, where God had placed and set me; and likewise for the ordering and governing of my children and family; so that we were willing both of us to live apart some years upon God's account and His truth's service, and to deny ourselves of that comfort which we might have had in being together, for the sake and service of the Lord and His truth. And if any took occasion, or judged hard of us, because of that, the Lord will judge them; for we were innocent. And for my own part I was willing to make many long journeys for taking away all occasion of evil thoughts; and although I lived two hundred miles from London, yet have I been nine times there, upon the Lord's and His truth's account; and of all the times I was in London, this last time was most comfortable, the Lord was pleased to give me strength and ability to travel that great journey, being seventy-six years of age, to see my dear husband, who was better in health and strength than many times I had seen him before. I look upon it, that the Lord's special hand was in it, that I should go then; for he lived but about half a year after I left him; which makes me admire the wisdom and goodness of God in ordering my journey at that time."

In connection with this subject, it should be remembered that George Fox, during his married life, was almost incessantly engaged in zealously propogating his views of Christian faith, and in establishing the religious society that grew out of them. As a Gospel minister he visited North America and the West India Islands; was twice in Holland, and other parts of the continent of Europe, beside long and laborious journeys in his native land, enduring also an imprisonment of fourteen months in Worcester jail.

Whilst his great mission remained unaccomplished, he contentedly relinquished the ease of a comfortable home, and the society of an interesting family. His industry and zeal were remarkable, love to God and love to man, and the interests of the beloved people, whom the Lord had enabled him to call from the barren and desolate mountains of an empty profession, to come and sit under their own vine and fig-tree, where none could make them afraid, were the powerful incentives that governed his conduct; and in the performance of his duty to his Divine Master, he was made willing to forsake not only houses and lands, but wife also, for His sake and the gospel.

At the expense of much time and patience, he frequently appeared before the Kings, Parliaments and Judges, in order to lay before them appeals for justice, mercy and moderation. He was also engaged with others in forming those excellent rules of discipline intended for the government of the society, in defending its doctrines from the arguments and cavils of opponents and apostates, and in writing and publishing books for these and other purposes.

London being the metropolis of the kingdom, the yearly meeting convening there, and many of the leading and influential Friends residing in that city, George Fox was necessarily much there in attending to the secular interests of the society.

The facilities for travelling of the present day strikingly contrast with the times we are now considering, scarcely any public conveyances being then in use. Stage-coaches were but just coming into existence in the reign of Charles the Second, and were slow, inconvenient and clumsy vehicles, with difficulty going the distance between Oxford and London in daylight, which is now performed in a little more than an hour. Travelling on horseback was commonly and almost universally practised; private carriages were used chiefly by the wealthier classes; and wagons carrying merchandise to different parts of the country also accommodated a few of the poorer sort of people. The state of the roads, also, at this period, formed a serious obstacle to the comfort of travelling, many of them being so much out of repair as to be almost impassable, and oftentimes infested with highwaymen; so that a journey of two hundred miles, beset with these difficulties, may form a very important reason why he was so much absent from home at this time.

It appears M. Fox again visited London, under religious concern, in the year 1698. At that time she addressed the following letter to King William, which was delivered to him by her daughter, Susan Ingram:—

"To King William:—

It hath pleased Almighty God to bring me unto this place, two hundred miles from my dwelling, in my old age (being entered into the eighty-fifth year of my age), to bear my testimony for that eternal truth, which I and many more are made partakers of, praised be the Lord; and I am not free and clear to return to my habitation, until I have cleared myself unto this government. I was exercised in this manner the first year King Charles the Second came to the crown, and laboured amongst them a whole year, to acquaint them, and give them to understand our principles, in giving letters and papers unto them for that end. And great opposition we had, both from church and state, yet it pleased God to cause them to give us some liberty to worship Him, though sometimes under great sufferings.

And now I am to acquaint King William, that we have been a people about forty-six years, and have lived under several reigns, and we have suffered very much, as it is well-known to the nation of England, even to the death of several hundreds by imprisonment and other hardships, and yet we were never found in transgression of any just or righteous law, but only upon account of our consciences towards God; that was the cause of our suffering, and not for evil or wrong done to any man or government; for our principle which we testify of is the Light of Jesus Christ, and His eternal spirit, which leads into all truth and righteousness, but not into any untruth or evil actions. And if any bearing the same name amongst us have transgressed against the precious truth and royal law of liberty, we do with the same spirit judge and condemn them wherever they are found. And we do deny all plottings and contrivings against the government, and all false and underhand dealing; and we live in that principle which is righteous, just and true; for God is a God of truth, and blessed are all they that fear Him, and walk in His truth. And now God has placed thee over us, in this government, who hast been very moderate and merciful to us, and we live very comfortably under thee and it, and do enjoy our meetings quietly, which formerly we were much disturbed in, which was a great suffering upon us; and God has blessed thy government, and prospered thy undertakings; for which the King and we have cause to bless His holy name, who is a God of peace, and His Son is Prince of peace, who now has given us peace and tranquillity, for which we praise His holy name; and thy gentle government and clemency, and gracious acts, God hath and will reward thee for. And as we abide in that just and righteous principle of the eternal God, by which we ought all to be guided, I hope the government shall never hear worse of us; but that we shall rather be a blessing than grievance to it and the nation; for so it will be as we continue in the blessed truth; in which I pray God for thy preservation, who am His servant, and thy faithful subject.

MARGARET FOX.

London, 24th of 4th month, 1698"

She died at Swarthmore, the 23d of the 2d month, 1702, in the eighty-eighth year of her age, having survived her husband about eleven years.

Her children say: "The blessed God of heaven and earth preserved her understanding to the last; and in the time of her sickness, she was in a sweet frame of spirit, and uttered many heavenly expressions near her conclusion in this world, which some of us were eye and ear witnesses of; and we believe she is inheriting a heavenly mansion, prepared by the Lord Jesus Christ, for all his faithful followers."

Thomas Dockrey, who visited her shortly before her decease, upon querying how she found herself, she answered: "Very weak in body, but alive in God:" he also heard her speak many comfortable and excellent words, thus: "The Lord is with me, and I am with the Lord, and in Him only will I trust and commit all to the divine providence of the Lord, both concerning my children and grand-children, and all things they do enjoy from Him, both in spirituals and naturals, who is the God of all the mercies and blessings to His people, throughout all generations: to Him be glorious praises forever. Amen:"

Her daughter expressing what a blessed mother she had been to her children, and whole posterity, she answered very sweetly: "Cleave to me, and you will not do wrong, for I am joined to the Lord."

At another time she said: "Oh! my sweet Lord, into thy bosom do I commit myself freely; not desiring to live in this troublesome and painful world; it is all nothing to me; for my Maker is my husband."

"Come, come, pray let us join the Lord, and be of one spirit, join to the eternal God, and be of one spirit."

At another time: "Come, Lord Jesus, I am freely given up to Thy will."

Again she said: "I freely forgive all people upon the face of the whole earth, for any wrong done to me, as freely as I desire to be forgiven."

And seeing her children sorrowful, she said: "Be quiet; for I am as comfortable, and well in spirit, as ever I was." And a little before her close, to her daughter Rachel: "Take me in thy arms, I am in peace."

She was interred in the burial-ground belonging to Swarthmore meeting-house, the 27th of 2d month, many Friends out of several counties being present. Thomas Camm, who attended her funeral, remarks: "The Lord did eminently appear with us, and many testimonies were borne to the honour of the truth, and great satisfaction to many there, of great quality and degree in the world; and to the comfort and edification of all the upright to God; to whom belongs the praise of all His wonderful works and marvellous loving kindness extended and multiplied, unto and upon His people, in and through our Lord Jesus Christ, world without end. Amen."

In the testimony of her children, concerning her, they say: "The Lord so increased her growth in the blessed truth, that she became a mother in Israel, and was very exemplary and serviceable in the church of Christ, strengthening the weak, and supporting the feeble. And a great care was upon her, and she was very diligent in speaking, and promoting the truth of our Lord Jesus Christ, both in this nation (where she travelled much), and to other nations by epistles: which care she performed and continued for many years, until the truth had made a larger entrance in the nations; discountenancing and reproving all false appearances, which would have made a show of that which they were not."

"And the Lord made her a preacher of righteousness, both in a public testimony for the truth, and in her life and conversation. And she continued her zeal and constancy to and for the truth, in her diligent attending of weekly, quarterly, monthly, and other meetings for worship, in which she was truly exemplary, to very near the conclusion. And also, she was raised up, and preserved a noble and valiant sufferer for the truth, and its innocent testimony; so she spared no labour nor pains, in travelling to visit those that were under confinement for the sake thereof, and was a comfort and strength to them therein."

Thomas Camm testifies of her: "And as she freely denied and despised the glory of this fading world, for Christ's and the truth's sake, God gave her honour, and a name amongst the righteous, with qualifications many ways for a considerable service in His church, in which she shined as a morning star, being filled with real wisdom and understanding, for the propagation of truth and righteousness; of a clear discerning of spirits, and the working of the enemy, to draw from the life and power of truth, into a liberty that genders to bondage, and to separation and breach of unity amongst Friends, appearing firm and zealous against the same, to the comfort and help of many; fervent and living in her ministry, and in supplications and prayers to Almighty God, to the edifying and building up many in that most precious faith, which gives victory over the world. Not only a great and exemplary sufferer for the truth, but a visitor and sympathizer with all the faithful in their sufferings, zealously labouring and endeavouring with such as were in authority for their relief, as being afflicted with the afflicted, and mourning with those that mourned, trusting in the Arm of God's power, which is the support of the righteous.

She never spared herself, nor doubted of good success, in her manifold labours on truth's account; both in her ministry abroad in most places in this nation, and other services: but approved herself such in zeal that needed not to be ashamed of her work and service for the Lord, His Truth, and people in her time, which she performed with all sincerity, and is now rewarded with the full fruition of eternal life, and peace with her God, whom she loved, feared and served with an upright heart, every way faithfully, while God was pleased to give her strength and ability to perform the same."

George Whitehead says: "She had a godly care upon her for the sober and virtuous education of her children and offspring; and the Lord blessed and answered her therein in a good measure, and no doubt blessed them the more for her sake, as well as for their own salvation, for which she chiefly travailed in spirit, and earnestly sought the Lord in their behalf, beyond all temporal blessings."

Beside the epistles addressed to Friends by M. Fox, she maintained an extensive correspondence with many of the leading and eminent persons in the society, in all parts of the nation. Numerous letters addressed to her are preserved in the Swarthmore collection, relating principally to the difficulties and persecutions under which many of its members suffered, and the various applications made to the monarchs, the Parliament and magistrates for redress. It is very remarkable to observe the respect with which she was regarded by the early Friends, and the affectionate terms in which they addressed her.

Edward Burrough styles her: "Dear Sister, who art a fruitful branch in the living vine, and a pleasant plant in the garden of God."

And Alexander Parker: "Dearly beloved sister,

dearly do I salute thee. Our life is one; our joy one; our suffering one; our food and raiment one; eating both of one bread, and drinking both of one cup in the Father's house, where there is bread enough, and wells of living water to refresh the tender plants; where the babes are nourished and fed with the milk, and receive their meat in due season; where there is joy and rejoicing in the presence of the Lord, and pleasures forevermore; which only those do enjoy, who have followed the Lamb through many tribulations and fiery trials and temptations, and have overcome by the blood of the Lamb, and their garments washed white and clean. Hallelujah! praises to His glorious name forever, who has called and chosen us, and made us partakers of the divine nature; and hath redeemed us from the world and the pollutions of it: to be witnesses of His powerful name; and in His power and free love, hath He sent us abroad into the world, to turn others from darkness and their vain conversation; that they may have union with us in the light of His Son, and praise and glorify His eternal Majesty forever and forevermore."

How much she was beloved by her immediate connections will appear from the following extract from a memorial of her by her sons-in-law, after her death: —

"And as for us, who are her sons-in-law, we cannot but give our testimony of our sense of her worthiness, and we account ourselves happy, and it is a singular mercy to us, that the Lord gave us wives of the daughters of such a worthy person, and that we are partakers of their virtuous education, whereby they are made a blessing to us," &c.

Indeed, she appears to have been regarded as a nursing mother in the church, both spiritually and temporally, visiting Friends in prison, entertaining them at her house, and freely dispensing of her substance for their comfort and support.

Thus having faithfully served her generation according to the will of her Heavenly Father, she has passed, we doubt not, to the fruition of that glorious reward promised to the righteous, to those who, through much tribulation, have washed their robes, and made them white in the blood of the Lamb.

EPISTLES.

PREFACE TO MARGARET FOX'S EPISTLES,

WRITTEN BY HERSELF.

FRIENDLY READER:—

The following epistles were written at the first appearance of truth among us, when we were young in it: the light of Christ being our first principle, our minds being turned to it, and it having become our teacher, leader and guider, we saw perfectly that there was no safety, nor preservation out of sin and transgression, but as we obeyed the light, and followed it in our hearts and consciences, it leading out of sin, transgression and iniquity: so as we waited in it, and dwelt in it, we came to witness a washing and cleansing, by the blood of Jesus. And so we came to discern, between the precious and the vile, and between the holy, and the unclean, and between the chaff, and the wheat; and between those that served God, and those that served Him not. And when we came to this sight, and knowledge, and discerning, then we became very zealous for God, and for His truth, and for the preservation of His people in the truth; and our hearts became tender, and we had a pity for all people's souls that remained in darkness. We were moved of the Lord to write often to Friends, and our testimony was very much to the light of Christ in the consciénce; because we saw that was the way, and there was no other; for Christ Jesus said, I am the Light; He also said, I am the way, the truth, and the life; and there is none that can come to the Father, but by me.

And so we received His Testimony, and could set to our seals that this was true. And then we saw the great concern that lay upon this, which is the salvation of poor people's souls. And we knowing as Christ said, they that hated the Light it was their condemnation; and also those that obeyed it, it would bring them to Christ their salvation; this made us very importunate with all people, both Friends and others, to direct them to the Light, and obey it.

And also there being such a body of darkness, which warred against it; for people having lived in darkness, out of the knowledge of the Light, it was such a new doctrine to them, that there was a mighty war in people's minds against it; and the priests and professors setting themselves against it, calling it a natural light; and some said it was a dim light, and some scoffingly called it a dark lantern, and others said it was not sufficient to condemn: so in their dark imaginations they fought against it. And very much we had to do in the beginning to get people convinced of the Truth, and of the sufficiency of it; and also those that were convinced, to keep them in obedience to it. But the Lord's arm and power carried on His own work, notwithstanding all the opposition of the power of darkness; glory and praises be to His holy name forever.

Here are a few epistles preserved, but many more are wanting, the copies being lost, with many other papers and letters that might have been serviceable; but in love to all people, we bring those that we have to open view; that if the Lord give a blessing to them, they may be serviceable hereafter, as they have been to many heretofore. The Truth is one and the same always; and though ages and generations pass away, and one generation goes and another comes, yet the Word, and Power, and Spirit of the living God endures forever, and is the same, and never changes.

And so, reader, cleave to the blessed Light and Truth of the living God, that He hath placed in thy heart, and believe in it, and hearken to it, and obey it, and it will lead thee in the path that we have gone, and then thou wilt see, and feel, and understand what we have gone through; and thou wilt come to be a witness of the living God and His Truth, which will be peace and comfort to thy soul.

The Lord God Almighty open thy heart, and enlighten the eye of thy understanding, that thou mayest come to have unity with all the saints in light.

A GENERAL EPISTLE TO FRIENDS, 1655.

Friends, whom the Lord God hath called unto the light which is eternal, which the Lord God has sent, to bring His seed out of bondage, and out of the house of darkness, from under Pharaoh, and his task-masters, which has so long been held under the dark power and mystery of iniquity. The Lord God of life and power hath visited you, and sent His servants to awaken you, and to raise you from the dead, that Christ might give you life, who is now come and coming to redeem Israel, and to divide the Red Sea, and to overturn Pharaoh and his host. Stand, still (I say unto you) and see the salvation of God, and in the fear of the living God wait low in your own measure of grace, and harken diligently unto that, that your souls may live. And this you must do, if ever you witness the living God; so in the name and power of the Lord Jesus Christ, at whose name every knee shall bow, and every tongue confess, beware how you spend your money for that which is not bread, and your labour for that which perisheth; it is the diligent hand that maketh rich, but the idle, slothful and negligent, suffer want. And beware of going from your Guide, which keepeth you low and tender, and prize the love of God that ever He should visit you; and beware that you do not requite Him evil for good, for He is a jealous God, and will not clear the guilty; it is the low, and the meek, and humble that the Lord God teacheth, it is the broken and contrite spirit, that God will not despise. And He, who is the high and lofty one, that inhabiteth eternity, dwelleth in the hearts of the humble.

But all who are got up in their imaginations, the Lord God will scatter, and the proud, the high, and the lofty, the Lord doth resist; and this you shall witness, the Lord feeds the hungry, but the rich is sent empty away. And they who thirst and breathe after righteousness, such the Lord satisfieth. So read, and with the eternal light examine and search, and try what it is that you thirst after; whether it be righteousness, purity and holiness, for these will the Lord satisfy; and whoever is not thus seeking, shall never receive satisfaction from the Lord God; but wrath, and terror, and horror, shall fall upon that which is contrary to this. So, as you love your eternal peace, and the redemption of your souls, keep low in your measure of the living testimony which cometh from the living God, which is one in all, in its measure one; there is no division, no rent, but all one. And this gathers your hearts together, and this knits and unites unto the body, where the unity is; and who gathers not here, scatters abroad; and he that is not with us here, is against us. So examine, and try whether you are gathering now or scattering abroad, with the Light which is eternal, which is one in all. Examine and try your own selves, I charge you, as you will answer it before the Lord God; come down and stoop to the yoke of Christ, which is easy, and take His yoke upon you, and His burden which is light; and beware of starting from under the yoke of obedience, or pulling away the shoulder; for the Lord God requires not only sacrifice, but obedience, which is better. And that mind that looks outward, from the measure enjoyed, and joins to anything without, contrary to the freedom of the spirit within, that mind is for judgment. The eternal spirit of God is one in all, and that which divides one from another, is for judgment, for where division is, that is of the kingdom that cannot stand. So read where you are, for if you are in that which is divided, you cannot stand. So in love and tenderness to your souls, I warn and charge you from the Lord, keep in the light, which is one, in the power, which is one, in the measure of life made manifest in you, which is one. And here is no division, nor separation, but a gathering and a knitting. And if you love the light, then you come to the light to be proved, and tried whether your works be wrought in God. But that which hates the light, turns from the light, and that shall be condemned by the light forever. And though you may turn from the light, where the unity is, and you may turn from the eternal truth; but from the witness of God in your consciences, (which he hath placed in you, which beareth witness for the living God,) you can never fly; that shall pursue you wherever you go. And they who turn out from the light, their resurrection is to condemnation, and on the left hand they are put among the goats, and shall have their portion with hypocrites and unbelievers; and this shall be witnessed forever.

And this I was moved of the Lord, to write to you, in love and tenderness to the measure of God in you, with which I have unity, which will witness for me forever; and this is in love to your souls. So the Lord God of life and power keep you alive in that, which He hath placed in you, to His everlasting glory: for a sweet savour we are unto God, both in them that are saved, and in them that perish. And beware how you draw back from the everlasting truth, that the Lord God hath tendered to you, which you shall eternally witness to be of God: *for he that draweth back, my soul hath no pleasure in him,* saith God. *That which we have heard, and have seen, and felt, and our hands have handled, even the Word of life which hath been declared unto you.*

From one who desires the good of all souls.

MARGARET FELL.

AN EPISTLE TO CONVINCED FRIENDS,

IN 1656.

DEAR FRIENDS, brethren and sisters in the eternal light, by which we are gathered, which is our teacher and leader: which light cometh from our Lord Jesus Christ, the Captain of our salvation, in whom is life, and this life is the light of men; who has laid down His life for His sheep, and who gives unto His sheep eternal life; and this life is in His Son: *your righteousness is of me,* saith the Lord; and this is the heritage of the saints: this you are made partakers of, who walk in the light, and dwell in the light, you shall have the light of life, and come to know the only true God, and Jesus Christ whom He hath sent, who is come a light into the world: he that believes in Him, shall not walk in darkness, shall not perish, but have everlasting life. And this is the Father's free love, to send His only begotten Son into the world, who is hated and rejected of men, but chosen of God and precious, who is become the head of our corner: glory eternal be to the living God! on Him are we built, in Him are we rooted and grounded: he is our foundation and root, we His offspring, on whom we stand fast, unmovable. This is the corner stone, which all the builders refuse and disallow; but on this rock is the whole church built, which is made of living stones, elect and precious, the spiritual temple, whose maker and builder is God. And now we having an *high priest over the household of God, let us draw near with a true heart, in full assurance of faith, having our hearts sprinkled from an evil conscience, and our bodies washed with pure water.* Wherefore return to the shepherd of your souls, an unchangeable priest which is made with an oath forever, after the order of Melchisedeck, who is made surety of a better testament, who needeth not daily to offer sacrifice, but he hath offered *one sacrifice,* and forever is set down at the right hand of God, from henceforth expecting until his enemies be made his footstool. For by one offering he hath perfected forever them that are sanctified; and of this the Holy Ghost is a witness to us in the fulfilling of the everlasting promise of the Lord God, who hath said, *I will put my laws in their hearts, and in their minds will I write them.*

Now, dear brethren, of this bear witness, and of the truth and faithfulness of the Lord God, you may set to your seals, all who abide in the light, and depart from iniquity, who name this name, which is better than other names: to which every knee shall bow, and every tongue confess. And now that ye are made partakers of a living, pure, eternal, immortal principle, which came from the living God, by which you may enter into the holiest, by the blood of Jesus, by this new and living way, which He hath consecrated for us through the veil (that is to say), His flesh: therefore hold fast the profession of your faith without wavering, for faithful is He that hath promised; and in the straight and narrow way that leads to life pass on, that through the straight gate you may enter, which few there be that find. Oh! in the eternal light (which is one in all) which leads up to the Father of light; and in the measure of light received from the Father and fountain of light and life, all wait, and dwell; and to the life raised by the immortal Word of life, join your minds; and pass from death to life, that so you may come to know and witness the true love that is to the brethren, where unity is, whereby you all may know that you are true disciples; in that you love one another; and here you fulfil the whole law, and keep the new commandment, which your Lord and Master has commanded.

Therefore, dearly beloved brethren, consider what ye are called to, and what ye are made to partake of, even of a living, and pure and holy priesthood, a peculiar people ye are, and of the holy nation, and of the Royal Seed. Now with the light which is eternal, which searches, tries, examines, weighs, and makes all things manifest of what sort they are; let it search and try you, how you grow up in the eternal and immortal birth, and do not deceive your souls: *For except you be born again, of water and of the spirit, ye cannot enter.* Now see whether ye can read this in the light; and whether ye know, and see, and witness this in your own particulars, yea or nay; and see whether you are not like Nicodemus, who said, *How can these things be?* and whether ye are not ignorant of this.

Therefore come down to the witness of God, and deal plainly with your own souls; and let the judge which stands at the door, pass sentence upon you. Let the time past suffice, that you have hid the talent in the earth, which you have received from the Lord to profit withal. And let the earth give up her dead, and the sea give up her dead, and hell give up her dead, and let all come to judgment; and let death and hell be cast into the lake; and freely give up that which is for the sword to the sword; and that which is for the fire, to the fire; so those who are dead in sin, may arise. For what avails it else, for you to take the profession and form of the living truth? *For if the dead rise not, ye are yet in your sins, and your faith is vain.* Therefore see what you are doing: for it is not the sayer, but he *that doeth the will of my Father;* and *many shall be called and few chosen.* Now see with the light which is eternal, that ye are not only of the many which are called, but of the few which are chosen; and give all diligence not to make only your calling, but your election sure. And Friends, your day of calling is come; ye are called out of the world, and separated from the world, by the call of the living God: the light calls out of Sodom and Egypt, where the many are. Therefore do not deceive yourselves, for ye are some of the many that are called; and ye are made partakers of that which calls continually, the voice behind, which cries, *This is the way, walk in it; why will ye die?* Now consider, how you hearken to this holy call, how you are obedient to it, how you are subject, and how you are taught and guided, by the measure of God's spirit; *for all the children of the Lord are taught of the Lord, and in righteousness are they established.* Now search with the light, which is eternal, whether ye are established in righteousness and purity; if ye are not, then mind the teachings of the Lord, *for he that walks in the light, as he is in the light, the blood of Jesus cleanseth from all sin.* Now examine whether ye are cleansed, whether ye are purged, whether ye are washed; for if ye walk in the light, then ye witness cleansing and washing.

Beware of betraying the just and the innocent in you (I warn and charge you, as you will answer it to the Lord) with a form and profession of the truth, without the life, and so betray your own souls; but to the pure eternal principle of the Lord God turn, and keep your minds unto this, which is given unto you, for the redeeming and ransoming of your souls from the captivity and bondage of sin and corruption; and hearken diligently to that of God that your souls may live; and that you may see your Saviour, who saves His people from their sins, and so witness the salvation of your souls. Ye are made partakers of the free grace of God, which brings salvation; so let it be your teacher and leader. And beware of turning this grace into wantonness, which is able to save your souls; but receive with meekness the ingrafted Word, that the milk thereof ye may witness, and as new-born babes, desire that you may grow thereby; and so the Word that is nigh, in the heart, which is the Word of faith which we preach; which Word was in the beginning (by which the heaven and earth were made), *which we have heard, which we have seen, which our hands have handled, this we declare unto you.* And to the measure of this in you, am I made manifest; and my joy and life is, that you would take heed to your own measures received, and be true and faithful to that which is able to save your souls; that eternal pure redemption ye may come to witness, and the unity of the faith, &c., and so joining to the body, which holdeth the head, from which the living virtue is received, you may grow up as lively plants in the garden of God, which he is dressing, watering, and pruning, that to Him fruit may be brought forth, who is the Lord of the vineyard, and the husbandman, who purgeth every plant that beareth fruit, that it may bring forth more fruit; and every branch that beareth not fruit, he taketh away. Now see with the eternal light, whether you bring forth fruit unto God; for every tree is known by its fruit; and every branch, which the Lord planteth, brings forth fruit (not only leaves, but fruit). Now search, whether you bring forth fruit or leaves; for that tree, that is in the garden, and brings forth nothing but leaves, is to be cut down.

Friends, deal plainly with yourselves, and let the eternal light search you, and try you, for the good of your souls; for this will deal plainly with you; it will rip you up, lay you open, and make all manifest that lodgeth in you; the secret subtilty of the enemy of your souls, this eternal searcher and tryer will make manifest. Therefore all come to this, and be searched, judged, led and guided; for to this you must stand or fall; and if you turn from this, it is a swift witness against the adulterer and sorcerer, and from it you cannot flee; in this I have cleared my conscience; for the good of your souls I have written, who desires that you all might be where I am, that so we might all be one. And so the Lord God of life and power keep you in His fear, that the Lord God you may serve and honour; that your hearts may be kept clean, and the secrets of the Lord ye may come to know, which none shall ever know, but those that fear Him; and this ye shall eternally witness. And therefore I say again, fear the Lord God, that so the pure wisdom ye may come to learn; for dreadful and terrible is the Lord God; and the day of the vengeance of our God is come, in which He renders to every one according to his deeds; the backslider, the revolter, the disobedient ones, the careless, the slothful, and those whose minds are at liberty, and will not abide in the cross of Christ; all these shall receive according to their deeds.

Therefore, dear Friends, abide in the cross, and keep your minds to that which is pure; so that you may come to witness the enmity slain, the handwriting of ordinances blotted out, and nailed to the cross, and you crucified to the world, and the world to you; and consider one another, and provoke one another to love and to good works; not forsaking the assembling of yourselves, but exhorting one another, and so much the more, as you see the day approaching. And dwell in love and unity, in the pure eternal light; there is your fellowship, there is your cleansing and washing. And here is the mystery to all the disobedient ones. And the everlasting God, of light, life and power, keep you all faithful to your own measure; that so the resurrection and the life ye may witness, and the living bread ye may feed on, which, whosoever eateth of, shall never die. So God Almighty be with you, and preserve you all faithful in Christ Jesus.

From your dear sister in the unchangeable love of Christ, who desires the good of all your souls.

MARGARET FELL.

AN EPISTLE TO FRIENDS, 1657.

Dear Brethren and Sisters, who are gathered in the light of Christ Jesus, the fountain of all light, and life, from whence light comes, from whence life comes, from whence power comes; which redeems out of nations, kindreds, people and tongues, to be kings and priests unto God, to reign with Him upon the earth. This is the possession of the saints who dwell in the light, that leads them into the life and fountain from whence it comes; here is the unity of the spirit, and bond of peace, which never can be broken. Here the pure language and worship of the Lord is, with one heart, one consent, and one soul, where there is no division; but the pure path of life is known, the way of holiness, where the unclean cannot pass, where the presence of the Lord is, wherein is fulness of joy, and pleasures forevermore. Now that every one may read his name here, in the unchangeable life is this written, that the pure life in all may prevail, and that the poor may receive the gospel; which is glad tidings of great joy to the oppressed and heavy laden, which groan under the bondage of corruption, and cry for deliverance; the cry whereof, is entered into the ears of the Lord of Sabaoth; and he hath determined in the thoughts of His heart, that the deliverer shall come from Zion, and the captivity of His people will He bring back, and salvation will come unto

Israel; so that Jacob shall rejoice, and Israel shall be glad, glory, everlasting glory be unto His everlasting arm forever; by which He gets unto Himself a name and victory even to the astonishment of the heathen, and to the confounding of His enemies, and to the recovering, raising and quickening of many who were dead in sins. And though He hath been a God unknown, now is He arisen in His light, which shineth in the conscience, and He hath caused it to shine out of darkness, and it hath shined in the heart; which gives the light of the knowledge of the glory of God, in the face of Jesus Christ His Son.

And now unto them who have long sat in darkness, and under the shadow of death, even unto them hath this light shined, who were sometime darkness, but now are they light in the Lord, who were dead in trespasses and sins, even them hath He quickened together with Christ, glory and praises be unto Him forever. Now dear friends in this quickening spirit, wherewith you are quickened out of the sleep and death of corruption, where Christ hath given you light, walk in Him, learn of Him, who is lowly, who is meek; and be swift to hear, slow to speak, slow to wrath, and keep down and baulk that part which receives a prejudice; search narrowly, and beware that you receive it not from a wrong spirit, for that will wrong the innocent; and the simplicity both in yourselves and others; it is hard to know the spiritual wickedness in high places, and it is with the spiritual weapons of the living God, that you can wrestle with the principalities and powers of spiritual wickedness; and it is the brightness of His coming, and the spirit of His mouth, that can reveal the man of sin, the son of perdition, that sitteth in the temple of God, exalted above all that is called God, showing himself as God. This is narrow and deep to discern between him that showeth himself as God, and is not, and him that is the true image indeed.

Dear Friends, this I write unto you in tender and in dear love to the Seed of God in you all, for which my soul travails; knowing and being acquainted with the danger of this spirit, which measures itself by itself, which the Apostle said was not wise, for such will boast of things without their measure, and will boast of other men's lines. Now that ye may know, and feel the life and power of every spirit; knowing the pure life in yourselves, you will come to savour it in others; and that which savours of the death, will be death to the life, in the fear of the Lord God. Beware of stifling the pure birth of God in you, and of wronging the pure innocent seed in you, which God is coming to plead the cause of in all flesh in this day. And beware that you join not with God's enemies, either in yourselves or others; but join with God's pure witness and testimony, and there will be your peace. And here you will know Him, who is the life, and the resurrection; he that believes in Him, though he were dead, yet shall he live; and there is no other name under heaven, whereby any shall be saved, than by that name, which is better than every name; to which every knee shall bow, and every tongue confess; but there are none that know this name, but he that hath the white stone, in which it is written.

From a true friend of the Seed of God in all nations. MARGARET FELL.

AN EPISTLE TO FRIENDS, 1659.

MY DEARLY BELOVED BRETHREN AND SISTERS, in the everlasting truth, and eternal love, and power of an endless life, into which we were begotten, and have been nursed up, and kept in, as living stones growing up in the temple of the living God; the same power and arm is present with you, and owns you; therefore keep in it, and let your faith stand in the power and life of God in every particular; and in that book of life will you read me near, as if present, in the everlasting covenant and bond of peace, which is never to be broken; and in that love of Jesus Christ, which none can separate us from, height nor depth, life nor death. The eternal God keep you, who brought again our Lord Jesus Christ from the dead, through the blood of the everlasting covenant; and by His blood wash you, and cleanse you from all sin, and all that would separate from God; that you may have fellowship one with another in the eternal light and life, and there I leave you; and to the Word of His eternal power I commit you, and commend you to His eternal Arm, which is able to save your souls, and to keep you up to Himself.

 M. F.

AN EPISTLE TO FRIENDS IN IRELAND,

IN 1661.

My dear love in the Lord God Almighty is unto you all, which never changeth, but endures forevermore; which love as it is lived in, preserves and keeps to the Lord God and His commandments, laws and statutes; which love is the fulfilling of the whole law of God, and answers to all commands, in thought, word and action. And this keeps clean, low and innocent, and moulds us into its own frame and temper, and so brings to be a new lump, leavened into the bowels of everlasting love, which reacheth unto all, and extends unto all, even unto enemies. Oh! blessed and happy are all they that are come into this sweet being of universal love, which would have all to be saved, and come to the knowledge of the truth. This is the image and nature of the blessed God, that holds forth His tender hand, and everlasting love, unto all people, nations, languages, kindreds and tongues, who is no respecter of persons, but every nation that fears God, and worketh righteousness, is accepted with Him, whose call is to every one that thirsteth, come, and whosoever is athirst, let him come and drink of the water of life freely. Oh! the infinite love and bowels of everlasting life and fulness that dwells in His blessed bosom, righteousness and peace is the habitation of His throne. Oh! my dear lambs, let the issues of life be kept open, that issueth into your souls, from this blessed fountain, that you may feel it always open unto you, and you open unto it, that you may always feel it fresh and new, flowing into your souls. So will you feel the word of the Lord God sweeter unto you than the honey, or the honey-comb; and so will you come truly to know, that man liveth not by bread alone, but by every word that proceedeth from the Lord God; here stands the life of men, and so to do the will of the Lord God, will be meat and drink unto you, and will be more delightful than your ordinary food; and then will not sufferings, trials and hardships be strange unto you; knowing that the Captain of your salvation, who is gone before you, is made perfect through sufferings; who in the days of His flesh, when He had offered up prayers and supplications; with strong crying and tears unto Him that was able to save Him, because He feared; though He was a Son, yet learned He obedience by the things which He suffered, and so must all that follow His steps; the servants are not greater than their Lord; and blessed and happy are all they that learn this lesson in the power of God, not only to believe on Him, but also to suffer for His sake; for they who suffer for Him, shall also reign over their enemies with Him; and in His power will they subdue and conquer at the last, for the Lamb and His followers shall have the victory.

And so, my dearly beloved, be strong in the Lord

and in the power of His might, and be faithful, and bold, and true to your Maker, and he will be a husband unto you, and set your feet upon the rock most sure, that if the storms beat, and the tempests blow, yet you will not be shaken, for He that keepeth you is greater than all, and none is able to pluck you out of His hand. Into whose arm and power I commit you, everlastingly to dwell and abide with the Lord God, with whom all things are possible. The God of love, whose mercies fail not, preserve and keep you all, and nurse you up in His own bosom, to His own praise and glory, that you may be a people saved by the Lord.

From your dear friend and sister,

M. Fell.

PRINCIPAL WORKS

OF

MARGARET FOX.

HER principal works are: "A Call to the Jews out of Babylon," addressed to Mannassah Ben Israel, a famous Jewish Rabbi, then in England.

"A Testimony of the Touch Stone for all Professors, &c., to try their ground and foundation by;" both published in 1656.

"A Loving Salutation to the Seed of Abraham among the Jews," &c.

"Women's Speaking justified, proved and allowed by the Scriptures, all such as speak by the spirit and power of the Lord Jesus," &c.

And "A Touch Stone, or Trial by the Scriptures of the Priests, Bishops and Ministers who have called themselves Ministers of the Gospel," &c.; besides numerous others of minor importance.

In "A Touch Stone, or Trial by the Scriptures," &c., she thus describes the nature, design and effect of true spiritual worship, and Christian ministry, which she contrasts with the dry, formal worship which so much prevailed among the professors of religion in that day:—

"Christ when he spake to the woman of Samaria, and she told him that their fathers worshipped in that mountain of Samaria, Jesus saith unto her, Woman believe me, the hour cometh, when ye shall neither in this mountain, nor yet at Jerusalem, worship the Father; but the hour cometh, and now is, when the true worshippers shall worship the Father in spirit and in truth, for the Father seeketh such to worship Him; God is a spirit, and they that worship Him must worship Him in spirit and in truth: and to this purpose Jesus spake unto Nicodemus, who came unto Him by night, when He said unto him, Verily, verily I say unto thee, except a man be born again, he cannot see the kingdom of God. At which words Nicodemus wondered; but Jesus answered, Except a man be born of water and the spirit, he cannot enter into the kingdom of God. That which is born of the flesh is flesh; and that which is born of the spirit is spirit. Marvel not that I said unto thee, ye must be born again; the wind bloweth where it listeth, &c.

And to this purpose was the man, whose name was John, sent of God, to bear witness of Christ Jesus the light, that all men through him might believe. He was not that light, but was sent to bear witness of that light, that was the true light, which lighteth every man that cometh into the world. He was in the world, and the world was made by Him. Which was born not of blood, nor of the will of the flesh, nor of the will of man, but of God. John bore witness of Him, and cried, saying, This is He of whom I spake, He that cometh after me, is preferred before me; and of His fulness have we all received grace for grace.

And to bring people to this light and spirit of the the Lord within them, did Christ Jesus and all His holy apostles endeavour by their preaching; therefore said Jesus Christ unto Nicodemus, We speak what we know, and testify what we have seen, and ye receive not our witness. This is the condemnation that light is come into the world, and men love darkness rather than light, because their deeds are evil. For every one that doeth evil hateth the light, lest his deeds should be reproved; but he that doeth truth, cometh to the light, that his deeds may be made manifest, that they are wrought in God. This is Christ's doctrine and worship.

"And when He was preaching among His disciples, and the Scribes and Pharisees heard Him, and many believed among the chief, but they did not confess Him, because of the Pharisees, lest they should be put out of the synagogue; Jesus cried out among them, and said, He that believeth in me, believeth not in me, but in Him that sent me. I am come a light into the world, that whosoever believeth in me, should not abide in darkness. And if any man hear my words, and believe not, I judge him not, for I came not to judge the world, but to save the world. He that rejecteth me, and receiveth not my words, hath One that judgeth him;

the word that I have spoken shall judge him at the last day.

"And Christ told the Pharisees that the kingdom of God came not by observation; but the kingdom of God was *within them.* And when He sent forth His disciples, He saith, As ye go, preach, saying the kingdom of God is at hand. Also when He sent out the seventy, He said, Heal the sick that are therein; and say the kingdom of God is nigh unto you. And we also see by the epistles of the apostles, which are left upon record, after what manner of doctrine and exhortation they spake unto the people. . . .

"When Peter speaketh of his beloved brother Paul and of his epistles, which he had written, and what he spake; some things, he saith, are hard to be understood, which they that are unlearned and unstable wrest, as they do also the other Scriptures, unto their own destruction. So they that have not the inspiration of the Almighty, and motion of the Spirit of the Lord God, the same that gave forth the Scriptures, when they come to interpret them, and give meanings to them, being unlearned therein, they just wrest them to their own destruction, and therefore they do not profit the people at all. These be they who separate themselves; men that are sensual, not having the Spirit. . . .

"Also the Apostle Paul in Romans, where he is speaking of his heart's desire and prayer to God for Israel, he tells them, That Christ is the end of the law to every one that believeth. For, saith he, the righteousness of faith speaketh in this wise, say not in thy heart who shall ascend into heaven, that is to bring Christ down from above? or who shall descend into the deep, that is to bring Christ up again from the dead? But what saith it? The Word is nigh thee, even in thy mouth, and in thy heart, that is the word of faith which we preach.

"And when he wrote to the Hebrews he rehearseth the new covenant, that the prophets Isaiah and Jeremiah had prophesied of, and saith, this is the covenant that I will make with them after those days, saith the Lord, I will put my laws into their hearts, and in their minds will I write them. These, with many more places of Scripture, might be instanced of the apostles, how they ministered both in preaching and writing.

"And in the first epistle of John, he saith, That which was from the beginning, which we have heard, which we have seen with our eyes, and our hands have handled of the Word of life: this we declare unto you, that ye may have fellowship with us; and truly our fellowship is with the Father, and with His Son Jesus Christ. Here was a right minister of God, that would have had those he wrote to, be in fellowship with him, who was in fellowship with the Father and with the Son; and therefore he saith unto them, these things I write unto you, that your joy may be full. This then is the message which we have heard from him, and declared unto you, that God is light, and in Him is no darkness at all. If we say we have fellowship with Him and walk in darkness, we lie and do not the truth; but if we walk in the light, as He is in the light, we have fellowship one with another, and the blood of Jesus Christ His Son cleanseth us from all sin. And again, the same apostle saith, A new commandment I write unto you; which thing is true in him and in you; because the darkness is past, and the true light now shineth. Let that, therefore, abide in you which ye have heard from the beginning. If that which ye have heard from the beginning shall abide in you, ye shall also continue in the Son, and in the Father. These things have I written unto you, concerning them that seduce you; but the anointing, which ye have received of Him, abideth in you; and ye need not that any man teach you, but as the same anointing teacheth you of all things, and is truth, and no lie; even as He hath taught you ye shall abide in Him: For ye have an unction from the Holy One, and ye know all things."

In "A Testimony of the Touch Stone for all Professors, and all forms and gathered Churches, &c., to try their ground and foundation by," she directs them to the light of Christ in themselves as a sure guide to holiness. A few extracts are given, to show her manner of treating the subject.

"Now is the light of the glorious gospel risen, and beautiful upon the mountains are the feet of them that bring glad tidings of this gospel, that publish peace, that say unto Zion, thy King reigneth. To all who desire to know the way to Zion doth this voice cry to turn their faces to the light of Jesus Christ, who came riding upon an ass' colt, to the joy and rejoicing of all Zion's children. Therefore turn again all you who are wandering from mountain to hill, seeking rest but finding none. Turn to the light in every one of your consciences; this is the word of faith which we preach, which Moses taught Israel, and the apostle Paul the Romans, which is nigh in the mouth, and in the heart. Here is your teacher, if you hearken to the pure light, which shows you the deceit of your hearts and your unclean thoughts, from which proceeds uncleanness which the light makes manifest, which will rip you up and reprove you in secret. The Lord God of life and power is fulfilling His everlasting covenant in this His day, He is writing His law in the heart and putting it in the inward parts, that none need say know the Lord, but all who turn to the measure of God shall know Him, from the least to the greatest of them. And by no other way or name under heaven shall ye know the living God, but by this pure light and law written in the heart. Here will ye come to witness the Lord to be your God, and your King, and your Law-giver, which all the professions of the world are ignorant of; therefore to this pure measure of God in your inward parts have your minds, that ye may come to witness cleansing and purging within, that ye may come to see the uncleanness which proceeds out of the heart, which defiles the man. For out of the heart cometh evil thoughts, murders, adulteries, fornications, thefts, false testimony, slanders; these are the things which defile a man.

And now you teachers and professors who look without you, and turn from this, which should cleanse within, how do you look that that which is without you, should cleanse from this uncleanness within? Let that of God in your consciences see how you can be cleansed by this, when ye turn from it. But if ye turn to the light which makes these things manifest, and dwell and abide in it, then will ye abstain from them, and so come to witness cleansing. For he that walketh in the light, as God is in the light, the blood of Jesus cleanseth from all sin. And Christ Jesus saith, A good man out of the good treasure of his heart, bringeth forth that which is good; and an evil man out of the evil treasure of his heart, bringeth forth that which is evil; for out of the abundance of his heart his mouth speaketh. And why call ye me Lord, Lord, and do not the things which I say? Whosoever cometh to me and heareth my sayings, and doeth them, I will show you to whom he is like; he is like a man which built an house and digged deep, and laid the foundation on a rock, and when the floods arose, the streams beat violently upon the house, and could not shake it, for it was built upon a rock. But he that heareth and doeth not, is like a man, that without a foundation built an house upon the earth, against which the streams did beat violently, and immediately it fell, and the fall of that house was great.

Now professors here's your building, eternally you shall witness this parable fulfilled upon you, the tempest and storms are coming, your house will be beaten down, it cannot stand, for you have been sayers a long time and not doers of the word; your house which you have built is without foundation, it is not founded upon the rock Christ Jesus. Ye who deny the light, He sayeth unto you, Why call ye me Lord, and do not the things which I say? upon Him shall ye be beaten to pieces, and all your profession. It is known and seen, ye are made manifest, ye cannot hide yourselves.

SWARTHMORE HALL.

THE following description, of the present state and appearance of Swarthmore Hall, is taken from Armistead's Select Miscellanies: —

"The Hall, though still a building of considerable size, is no longer what it once was; a large portion having become ruinated has been altogether removed; the oriel window from which George Fox preached to the people in the orchard still remains, and it is believed the owner of the property is bound to accommodate any travelling Friend with a bed. The hospitality of the Friends of Ulverston, however, prevents this right being demanded; and no instance has been known within memory, of any Friend exercising his privilege. The old *bedstead* bequeathed by George Fox, used to be kept here, and may possibly still remain. The room in which Friends held their meetings for the first forty years, and which were generally graced with the attendance of George or Margaret Fox, and others of the society's parents in Christ, remains in its pristine state, having an embrasured window, and a raised dais at one end, which served for a minister's gallery.

The situation of the Hall is somewhat singular and picturesque. Eastward of it, to the bay of Morecambe, extends a tract of rich champaign country, rivalling for beauty, wood and fertility any county in England; the Swarthmore Hall estate formerly comprised much of this. Westward extends the bleak tract of Swarthmoor recently enclosed, but still strongly contrasting with the rich pasture of the opposite view. Northward may be discerned the town of Ulverston, and beyond the pointed mountains of Coniston and the Lake district. The immediate neighbourhood of the Hall is occupied by an ancient grove of forest trees, partially screening from view the barren common, while at the foot of the orchard is a woody dell, through which a stream murmurs over its pebbly bed.

The meeting-house is a solitary building, a quarter of a mile from the Hall; it is entered in the good old-fashioned way, through a porch, with a bench on each side, and over the door the inscription: Ex dono G. F., 1688 (the gift of George Fox, 1688). It is commonly supposed he used to attend this meeting. Such, however, is not the case; he never sat in it, being in the south of England from its completion until his decease. It was, however, built at his cost, and on land given by him — the only piece of land he ever possessed in England. On entering the passage leading forward from the porch, two black ebony pillars, plain and slender, are seen, one on each side, supporting the ceiling. They are sometimes called George Fox's bed-posts, and rightly so, being the posts of the bedstead mentioned before. It was considered the best way of preserving the two principal posts, as well as to bring them under the notice of strangers, to place them in this situation. Then there are also two massive arm-chairs, of solid oak, adorned with carved work; they belonged to George Fox and his wife, and were removed hither from the Hall.

Adjoining the meeting-house is the burial-ground, which is somewhat modern. The old burial-ground lies at Sunbreak, about a mile and a half distant, and is to many a spot of peculiar and intense interest. It is at the edge of a barren moor, the higher part of which consists of naked limestone, and at the highest point of all is the remains of a beacon. About a third of a mile south of this beacon, where the cultivated land begins, is a small enclosure, surrounded with an eight foot wall, and entered by a low, narrow door. This, for about the first seventy years of the society's existence, was the burial-place belonging to Swarthmore meeting.

Here lie the remains of many that braved persecution and suffering for conscience' sake, and so obtained for us the privileges we enjoy. Many valiants in the cause of truth have here been laid, when freed from the troubles of time; amongst them lie the remains of Margaret Fox, emphatically a mother in Israel, whose sufferings were rendered more poignant from previous affluence, her body imprisoned, and her estate premunired, yet her noble spirit remained unbroken."

THE END.

www.ingramcontent.com/pod-product-compliance
Lightning Source LLC
LaVergne TN
LVHW021428110826
845150LV00007B/2128

9781425507701